To ∂ B + B.
Enjoy

Flo Hamish
12-24-06

A Psalm of Joy and Lamentation

A Wife's African Memoir

A PSALM OF JOY
AND LAMENTATION

Library of Congress Number: 2006905978
International Standard Book Number: 1-932864-90-3

Cover Information
Painting of Mama Rosi
by Florence Rheinheimer Harnish, 1969

Printed at
Masthof Press
219 Mill Road
Morgantown, PA 19543-9516

DEDICATION

This memoir is dedicated to
David M. Harnish, my husband,
our children, Marie, David Rollin, and Anne,
and Mary Jane Lederach
and Hiram Hershey.

Contents

FOREWORD

In my mind I have written this "memoir" many times since the years we were in Tanzania, East Africa. I am a changed, grateful person for having the privilege to have been a person who has lived in another culture from the years 1967 to 1970. The memories of those wonderful/ terrible years is very vivid in my mind, and have influenced my life and thought ever since.

Why did I write it? It seemed necessary to me, for me, for our children, because Janie suggested giving my letters to the historical society, and to let friends and family know what experiences have contributed to making me the person I am today.

Our family was sent to East Africa, under the umbrella of Mennonite Central Committee's (Akron, Pennsylvania) Teacher's Abroad Program (TAP) as something of an anomaly—my husband Dave and I were not teachers in a school ,but a doctor and a nurse.

In the letters, which became less frequest as the years passed, my reactions to happenings, places, people, concepts, changed. For the better, it is to be hoped. Although we had some trying experiences, I would not give up those experiences. At the same time, neither would I like to repeat some of them. I feel extremely privileged to have been allowed to be in contact with a culture and a beautiful people in Africa. To have learned a language, worked and lived as a woman amongst women of a differing culture is a gift, par none. I never wanted to be known, while I was in Africa, or since, as a "missionary." It doesn't seem right to me to this day to want to change people's thinking, but rather, to be privileged to be their friend, whatever their religious persuasion. I have often wondered whether the experience of being there was as beneficial to the persons I encountered, as it was to me.

Some notes on the letters may be helpful. The letter to Elaine Unzicker was at her request, in anticipation of working in East Africa, also, accompanied by their small children. The letter to the Ashleys in Brazil, written by both Dave and me, is because we had been friends at Goshen College, Goshen, Indiana; Margaret Brubacher Ashley was a nursing colleague and classmate of mine at Goshen College; the letter to Mrs. DeTuerk was in response to a package sent by the DeTurks (Dr. DeTurk was a colleague of Dave's).

Above all, I am grateful to Mary Jane Lederach Hershey ("Janie") to whom I wrote so many letters. She must have been my confidant; I wrote things to her that I would not have written to my parents. Janie and Hiram supported us, when there seemed no one else doing so. My letters to her are full of thank you's for all the things they sent to us for our personal use, as well as for my use in relating to the women of the culture in which we were living, and to others. She has been a good friend ever since 1948, when we were both beginning students at Goshen College. She was a good listener, and, although I did not include them in this memoir, wrote me many wonderful letters, and attempted to keep us abreast of the news happenings of the day, Stateside. She saved all of my letters to her, and interestingly enough, I had made copies of those I typed to her, and saved them as well. So the written correspondence exists today.

Janie and I were rearing children in those years, and a lot of our verbal interactions, relate to that fact, as is evident in the letters. Dave and I had been living in Philadelphia, and Hiram and Mary Jane in Harleysville, PA since the time Dave and I got married in 1956, and had spent a lot of time discussing various child-related issues. Also, breastfeeding had been highly discouraged stateside n the years preceding our stay in Africa, so we spent some of our energies discussing this matter also. Women were more or less succeeding and/or failing at this most important task, largely due to a lack of feminine support, as well as instructions from physicians: "Your baby will grow faster if you give him/her milk from a bottle." Dave and I knew this concept was prevalent, and, because he was a doctor, we had scads of free baby formula given to us when our children were born as well as Dave being taught that way in medical school. Fortunately, as a nurse, I was able to resist some of these teachings. Being in Africa where breasts were used so openly to feed children, as nature intended, also reinforced my ideas of the importance of breastfeeding.

As for the journal entries, I have tended to journal through, or about, crises in my life, thus the chapters on "digging" and "snakes", etc., came to be while we were still in Tanzania.

The vignettes have been written from the vantage point of thirty some years heaving passed. My memries may have been ameliorated by being softened, hardened, forgotten, remembered from a single viewpoint, or by other factors. To the reader, please forgive me for this, but it seems unavoidable.

I hope the reader of these letters, journals, and thoughts, can forgive me for repeating myself at times. I truly did intend to be truthful and factual, and I trust that those persons whose names are mentioned are not offended that they are included; and if they are offended, I beg their forgiveness.

DEFINITIONS

aayah - nursemaid to a child

bilharzia - a serious liver disease caused by flukes living in stagnant water

bwana - Mister

choo - toilet

CMS - Christian Medical Society

dawa - any drug or medicine or substance

dresser - medical worker

fundi - expert

kanga - cloth used as head or body covering by women, and to carry a baby, usually on the back

kiswahili - has same meaning as swahili

kumbe - an exclamation that can mean many things, depending on how and when it is said. Something like the way Americans might say "oh".

MTS - Menno Travel Service

mzungu - white person

rondavel - a round hut
safari -   any trip, long or short
Shirati -   Mennonite Hospital and Mission
                 Station in nothern Tanzania.
sufarini -   large pot
uhuru -   freedom
ujamaa -   freedom
wazungu -   plural, white persons

INTRODUCTION

*W*hy did I, we, go to Africa at the time we did? Good question.

For one thing we felt like our lives were just starting. At the time we were contemplating going to Africa, or to some other voluntary service project, we had heard some appeals from Mennonite Central Committee (MCC) and Eastern Mennonite Missions (EMM) for people to go overseas. By the time we seriously considered going, we had three children, and Dave had finished his surgical residency to become a surgeon. Some physicians had returned stateside to become surgeons, having spent a stint overseas and encountered the need to operate for illness and emergencies for which they were not prepared, so we decided it wisest to go with Dave already a surgeon. We made this decision together.

We are both followers of Jesus and we wanted to bear witness to this fact. My faith and joy in the faith has grown exponentially, since that time, though not without times of doubt and searching. I never wanted to go as a "mission-ary" because for me, an imbalance occurs between persons when one of them attempts to change the other person's way of thinking and believing. For me it was important that we be "volunteers," as opposed to "missionaries," and the entire time we were in Tanzania, I maintained that position. Both of us are members of the Mennonite Church and do not believe in using military force to obtain a goal. Yet I was always transfixed by the fact that young soldiers sacrificed their relationships with their loved ones and even their lives, for causes they felt were just. After Dave had finished his surgical residency, he had the beginnings of a practice in Philadelphia with one of his colleagues, and was becoming Board Certified in surgery. But we had always felt that since Dave had missed the draft for I-W (conscientious objection) service, by farming, or being a student, it would behoove us to do something constructive, rather than participate in the destructiveness of war, as a military service would have been.

Another reason for us to go overseas was for the sheer adventure of it. To live in another country and culture seemed quite alluring. To boot, we would be able to help people!

But this book is primarily about my own experiences, so why did I go? Traditionally speaking, wives go where their husbands go — at least this was a commonly accepted behavior in the 1960's. When I got married, I moved from my family in Indiana with barely a glance backward, to be with Dave in Philadelphia. To follow Dave seemed easy at the time, though there were many occasions when I wished I could have been able to see my family back home, talk to them, help them, and have other interactions with loved ones. That was in the day of few telephone calls, because of the expense, and only a few letters now and then. Holidays were especially hard, in Philadelphia, as well as in Africa. I have one deep regret which is that I was not present at my parents' 50th wedding anniversary. In hindsight, I think I should have flown home for that. But it did take me a long time to grow up in my relationships, and I am still working at it.

Also, I wanted to do some good in the world, as a nurse. I had been teaching nurses and assumed there would be a position for me wherever Dave and I went.

I also thought as a nurse and doctor married to each other we would be able to work together and I could be closer in actuality to Dave. His having been in medical school in our early marriage required a lot of study and little free time for him. To teach nursing required the same expenditure of time for me. We loved each other, then as now, and we wanted to be together. Later I realized that there are always stresses on a family, and we encountered stresses in our lives after Africa too, in Philadelphia, Akron, and Ephrata, in places that we lived.

But the experience of being overseas was, for me, some-what ironic, in light of the decision making process. It would surely have served us well to have been able to have some counseling and advice prior to our departure. And certainly, it would have helped to have a body of persons, Christians, a church, or someone to offer support, although Hersheys were very, very supportive.

When it was time for orientation with MCC, Dave felt he couldn't take the time to go. We had offered to volunteer with both MCC and EMM. In the Teacher's Abroad Program (TAP) there seemed to be a place for us. Dave had preferred to go to an English speaking country, although to me, it did not appear to be an obstacle to learn a foreign language. Dave would particularly have liked to go to Shirati Hospital in Tanzania, because he had an aunt, Mary Harnish, who was a missionary nurse there. For me, wanting to go as a nurse, to work together with my physician husband, to a needy country overseas, it did not seem too important where we went. However, seeing the word "doctor," particularly "surgeon," seemed to outweigh the word "nurse" when we were being given our assignment.

Since Dave wanted to go to Shirati Hospital, we were told by both EMM and MCC that they did not need "doctors" there. I recall no mention whatsoever of "nurses." We were told that we, i.e., the "doctor," would be secunded to the Lutherans, who desperately wanted a doctor at Ilembula Lutheran Hospital, and had been praying for one. There was no discussion of the nursing situation at Ilembula, or any place else, that I can recall.

Since the entire experience of going overseas had been a bittersweet one for me, I have given much though to it. I was a person eager to go on a volunteer assignment, but I was not given an assignment. When we got to Ilembula, the nursing school was fully supplied and funded with personnel from Scandinavia and Germany, and later from Holland. There seemed to be no opening for a person with my credential (I was a nurse, and had been teaching nursing). One time only, was I asked to be part of the nursing teaching process in Tanzania, and that was to give some exams in bedmaking. Bedmaking is one of the beginning skills in nursing, and I did not consider it be terribly important. I did, however, participate, and as best I can recall, I gave every student a 100%. Perhaps that is why I was never invited to participate again!

I preferred to work in the hospital. There were no other Americans living closer than 60 miles away. Why would MCC send a couple with three young children to such a remote place? No one for us to talk to, and I was often lonely. I was the only *mzungu* (white person) there who did not have an assignment. One of the Tanzanian women asked me about that one time. I would have had much more house-hold and child care help there than I could have had state-side. I got into a situation overseas in which I was not able to fully participate in nursing and this was a source of frustration to me—and led to some unhappiness there. However opportunities to work one-on-one with other women were opportunities I may not have had, had I had a more specific assignment.

There was never an opening for me to work, nor chance to go to the villages in the Landrover to give immunizations and do health teaching. As my Kiswahili improved, I made some effort to teach medical things to the *wanawake* (women). I particularly remember their eagerness to hear how to prevent having children. Mortality rates for young children were around 50%, and polygamy was being practiced. So there was definitely a vested interest in issues surrounding children and childbirth. I recall hearing that women who were in polygamous marriages were permitted to join the Lutheran Church in Ilembula, but that the males were not. Since we were not intimately involved in these matters, however, this was just hearsay.

My intent in writing these things, is to state the truth, without gloss. These were happenings as I recall them. I feel that oversight, friendship, and consultation would have been very helpful to us in our overseas assignment. For whatever reasons, since we were "anomalies" under the Teacher's Abroad Program, we seemed to have fallen through some oversight cracks. We were on our own, basically, bringing our own unadulterated culture with us. Our experience in Tanzania was a wonderful/terrible one. I would not exchange that world view changing experience. Of course, how can how can exchange one's experiences in life? We can only examine them, and create the best or worst of them. I am privileged to have been allowed to go to Africa, to meet wonderful, beautiful people. The experience would have been better? Worse? Under different circumstances? Only God knows.

LETTERS

1967

Postcard addressed to:

Mr. and Mrs. Hiram (Janie) R. Hershey

June 1967
London, England
Tues. 10:30 P.M.

Dear Hersheys,

Arrival here 7 A.M. London time, 2:30 A.M. Philly time, therefore were very tired today, but still managed to see quite a few things—Buckingham Palace Guards, Westminster Abbey, ducks, and other buildings Dave could tell you about but I don't know the names of. We are in one room, 4th floor, walk-up (all those suitcases!). Tomorrow on to Rome by plane. The ride was very smooth. Everyone cheerful tonight, but not so all day!

Love and thanks,

Harnishes

Friday, June 30, 1967
Shirati Hospital
Tanzania, East Africa

Schedule here: (DAILY!)
7:30 – Breakfast
10:00 – Coffee
1:00 – Lunch
4:00 – Tea (for all missionaries)
7:00 – Dinner

Dear Janie,

So much has happened to us since we saw you at the airport. Right now we are here at Shirati at Aunt Mary Harnish's house. We've been here since Tuesday evening. It is nice here. The weather is almost perfect . . . The days are warm, a little hot over siesta time, but cool enough for cover at night. We have seen a lot of the Housmans, Dick and Ruth Weaver (whom we knew in Philadelphia), Elsie Cressman (remember her from Goshen?), and the other missionaries, since the houses are very close together. They are taking turns having us to their homes for the main meal in the evening, breakfast we eat here, and lunch with Elva Landis another missionary. We plan to go on down to Ilembula from Musoma next Tuesday. Musoma is apparently another mission station (no hospital) with mostly teachers. The road from Musoma to Shirati is about 75 miles over a true dirt, washboard, pothole road, and at one point we crossed a river by ferry, car and all.

After we left London on Tuesday the 20th, we went to Rome on Alitalia. The planes are nice, except it's hard for the children to stay put. They're always feeding you. In Rome we went touring quite a bit. I had always thought of Rome as the Vatican City, but it was the ruins that really impressed us. The Coliseum and some of the old temples and such are truly magnificent. The catacombs are quite unbelievable. I guess if someone was feeding me to the lions I would be able to live and work there too, but it is very difficult to conceive of it. They are quite extensive, with several layers connected by steps, all carved out of rock and dirt. Monks or priests (or somebody like that) in long frocked robes took us on tours there. We also went on the old Appian Way, and saw a lot of other stuff that I haven't remembered since I took history courses someplace or other. The airport lost our stroller in London. I am just sick about it every time I think about it, because I had gotten it especially for traveling. I am going to do all I can to recover it. In Rome we rented a stroller for two days, and then I felt much more like I could function. We were almost immobilized with three small, very tired children until we got that stroller. Anne slept in bureau drawers in London and Rome. Either babies don't go touring, or more likely, sleep with their parents. One lodging place told us the parents brought their own bed for babies. (I tried.) We have not been sick in the least little bit so far, for which we are extremely grateful. Dave had brought along a well-stocked medicine bag in case we were, but the only thing we needed from it were anti-malarials.

Almost all of the missionaries here have cooks, cleaning personnel, laundry personnel—either one or all three. My first impressions are that this is a much more leisurely pace than that which I have been leading at home. The wives are quite free to do all the sorts of things that one would wish to do in America but can't. There are only small children here, because the others are away at boarding school. I guess the Housmans are really the only ones. Their little Heidi (4 years) is the oldest one here. There are a lot of African children around, but from what I can gather, the missionaries' children don't play with them. They live in little houses here and there. I haven't had a complete tour of the place yet. Right now it is nearly 12:00, and Lois, Aunt Mary's servant, is cleaning the floor. She did some laundry for me, washed our dishes every day. Mary does her own cooking (unlike anyone else, I think) but at noon she eats with Elva. The meals are good, but David and Marie are turning up their noses at some strange mixtures we have had, as well as papaya and mangoes, although David eats fresh pineapple like crazy. The baby is eating like a horse as usual. She has been unusually happy this whole trip. I have been glad over and over that I decided to continue nursing her—especially in Rome. She is walking around furniture now, and is happiest when standing.

We may be able to take language at Nairobi in September. The Lutherans are strongly considering it. Right now I can see why. All the Swahili I can say is good morning, and thank you, and as for the rest I can smile, period! No communication at all.

Safari ants on the move.

The first night we were here we were invaded with safari ants. Until this has happened to you it is difficult to conceive of the situation, but I was ready to return to Philadelphia! Mary, Dave, and I were **sweeping** them out the door. There were millions of them—big black biting ones. I have heard that they can kill a stuporous person, or a baby if they are in their way. Mary said it adds to the story! Everyone here seems to take it quite casually, but I was not able to. Ruth Weaver says they were awakened one night by their **biting** them in bed, and they had swarmed all over the house except their baby's room (thank goodness), and they returned three nights in a row! She was ready to go home too! Anyway they're gone, and I'm thankful that Aunt Mary was with us when this happened. Some time ask me for more details if you're that interested. Also on the negative side, David is covered with mosquito bites in malaria country. We have now rigged up mosquito nets. We don't think there is malaria where we are going, but we're not sure yet.

The Housmans are going on furlough in a matter of weeks. I hope you can see them. We had some delicious Victoria Lake fish with them last night, curried, and Harold demonstrated how to eat the heads. Please ask him to demonstrate how to eat the eyes and brains if you have a chance. Also played a game of tennis last night, and scrubbed for an operation Harold was doing on a man's eyes. Rather reassuring to find that I still know how after about 12-13 years! It's dangerous to walk into the hospital, they put you to work. We are eager to hear all the news.

Love, Flo

I was so frantic about those ants that when I pulled out a little stand to clean them away from behind it, something from the top of the stand fell and broke. I have had to live with the fact that I broke a souvenir that Aunt Mary Harnish got in India while she was there learning how to make artificial legs for leprosy patients.

LETTERS

1967

August 3, 1967
Ilembula, Tanzania

Dear Janie,

In my mind I have told you a million things about all of the things we have been doing and seeing, but of course we are no Jean Dixons and have no mental telepathy! Sometimes I really feel the need to talk to someone at home and tell them everything. I guess this is part of "adjustment." We are here at Ilembula now. We arrived here on July 4, but we did not hear the *Star Spangled Banner*. We were met at the airport by a number of dignitaries of the local church and the Lutheran Church at large (German primarily). (I see I set my margins too wide! I am typing with a Swedish nurse's typewriter and it has things like this å ä ö § etc., where I normally have . , : ; so don't be surprised.) Anyway, these 13 men who met us at the airport took us into the regional Lutheran office and we had "tea" and speeches with translators. We had just gotten off the airplane, looked a mess, and David had been airsick between Mbeya and Njombe (pronounced N-jom-bay), where we got off. I asked the Finnish secretary (the only woman present) to take me to the bathroom which turned out to be a cemented hole in the ground! Later we went to the Lutheran missionary's house in Njombe where there was every modern convenience.

Then over **dusty** (in clouds) roads, with marvelous scenery, to Ilembula with two Germans who spoke heavily accented English. Here we hear English with German, Swedish, Finnish, Danish, and Swahili accents. All I can say is thank heavens it's English. Since we are here, we urgently feel the need to learn the Swahili language. You simply cannot talk to anyone but the missionaries and a few educated Tanzanians. In fact we are being sent by the Lutherans to Language School in Nairobi, from September 12, 1967, to December 8, 1967, (Mennonite Guest House, P. O. Box 7596, Nairobi, Kenya) in order to learn Swahili. I'm really glad, because unless you make a **very** conscious effort it would be exceedingly difficult to learn it in everyday discourse.

Here there are a German doctor, his wife, their 18-month-old daughter, and their 18-day-old son, and about half a dozen nurses from various countries, as mentioned above. The missionary here at Ilembula (Ee-lem-boó-la) is Swedish and is on furlough now—in fact we are living in their house and using most of their things. They have children ranging in age from 7 years down to 1 year (five of them) so we are looking forward to their return in September. When we get back in December we will be living in another house here, very similar to this one although only two bedrooms whereas this is three. The house from the outside looks like a modern brick house, one-story high. We have as follows:

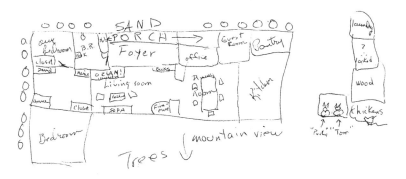

The rice always had tiny bits of stones in it. I have heard of several *wazungu* (white people) who have broken teeth on the rice, if the little stones were not sorted out. It was hard to get all the stones out.

I have had a lot of trouble mentally about this meat. It seemed so cheap to me, but the Tanzanians were not able to afford it, and we bought it even for our dog!

I am trying to get this in tonight's mail, so I must hurry. It goes out twice a week. My husband tells me it's the 27ᵗʰ of July instead of the above date, so you can see I'm a bit mixed up as to time! We have a wood stove (!), and I have been baking bread like mad. I like to experiment and have tried nearly all of the bread recipes in *Joy of Cooking*. The "whole wheat bread plus" is my favorite so far. The rice must be sorted out, tiny potatoes peeled, meat cooked for an entire day to taste like delicious beef (we have it delivered to the door for 17 cents a pound and think it must be oxen—we wash our hands carefully after handling it), buy milk at the door—10 Shs./ month for a liter a day, must be boiled immediately (dubious sources and dubious dilutions), and these trees grow here: orange, lemon, papaya (**something** like ripe cantaloupe and delicious) plus some other fruits that we don't know the names of yet.

David, Anne, and Marie soon after arrival in Ilembula.

Our diet is not too varied as yet, but we hope to grow our own things when we get back from Nairobi as some of the others do. The children have two white rabbits, are getting tan, play in the sun and sand all day long, almost like living at the beach. They seem to like it very well here. We have electricity all day and night except for the afternoons, cook on a wood stove, the laundry must be done by hand (white things are boiled in huge pots).

We have an African girl working for us and I am extremely grateful for her help. The women here do their own cooking and baby tending (unlike the Mennonites at Shirati), and I will give you more details another time. We are healthy and think we will like it. Hospital is quite antiquated. Hello and love to all. What are you doing? Vacationing, camping, swimming, etc., no doubt. This weather is something like Cape Cod weather—blankets at night, too hot to stay in sun at noon.

Marie, Anne, David Harnish playing with sand in front of Harnish house.

Love,
Flo & family

P.S. I didn't have time to re-read this. We have tap water (cold in tub), must be boiled for drinking.

August 17, 1967
Ilembula, Tanzania

Dear J. & H.,

Why I am writing to you again when I should be writing to other people I am not sure, but I think it's so I don't have to study Swahili. You know all the gambits of getting out of something! Besides, Dave wrote a letter to Hiram the other day and didn't leave any space for me; you know I always

If a baby cried, since it was usually being carried on the back of the mother, she simply swung it around and let it suck. Being an American, and not having the kind of freedom and wisdom to carry my baby on my back that way, and swing it around to suck, I used a pacifier. During the time I sang with the Ilembula Women's church choir, they did the same; *i.e.*, swung the baby around so it could suck. Americans have made something of breasts other than what God intended—to nourish a baby.

have to have my say! We got a letter from the Hogges. Louisa had quite a scare.

Marie's message to Peter and Tom: "Tell them I am going to save some candy for them." David's message to Jim: "I'm playing in the sand. And something else, I'm playing with blocks [from the woodpile]. And something else, I'm playing with my shubbel. And something else, I'm playing with Tiki." Tiki is a dog here to whom David has become quite attached. Her owner is a Swedish nurse who will be going on furlough in September and we are going to have the dog as ours when we get back from Nairobi in early December. To best describe her I would say that she looks like a miniature "Lassie." Now in this house, we have sort of a shaggy mutt named "Nolly." Anne stands alone freely, if coaxed, takes a few steps—rather remarkable since she only began creeping at 8 months! She is into everything now. Do say "hello" to all of our mutual friends. Dave is learning to play the alto recorder and we can play a few simple duets together in the front part of Katz. I'm brushing up on soprano. How's yours? How was music camp? Have you seen Housmans? Please stay in our house overnight if necessary for your Philadelphia activities.

Sometime (in a spare moment) read *How to Raise Children at Home in Your Spare Time* by Gersch, and let me know if it's worthwhile having. I tried to get it before we came. Also I did like Ginot's: *Between Parent and Child.*

The German doctor's wife here lets her newborn "cry it out" between feedings—she's "teaching" the baby. I am sold on the pacifier when I see how the Africans do it—it's second best.

Life here has not become humdrum. Last week a Mrs. Fox, the wife of a tea plantation foreman, came here to deliver her third child. Here all the babies are delivered by midwives with the doctors assisting only in complicated cases and Cesareans. Two weeks before her delivery she was "tossed" by a cow. This was their third boy and the old-

David playing with Kiki.

est is 3-1/2. She teaches 18 or so children on their plantation from ages 3 to 8 and we had some very interesting discussions regarding early learning. She was walking up and down these hills on the second day as though nothing in the world had happened to her. Of course out here everyone nurses their babies without question.

We would like to visit their tea plantation sometime, perhaps this weekend. They are from England and have been here for 5 years; unless he is promoted soon the Tanzanian government will not extend their visas. They are located in a rain forest, at 6,000 feet, it is very cold, and they even have frost sometimes. (In this tropical country!)

The latest experience we had I must tell you about. On Tuesday of this week L_____, the German nurse who seems to be in charge here, said there was an American girl at our house who wanted to "rest." (There is a constant stream of European visitors, usually missionaries and their families, who come to Ilembula to see the doctor. This is a very **modern** hospital for these parts!)

Anyway, I went home and an attractive 25-year-old, American Peace Corps girl from Detroit was there. She had **walked** 7 miles over an African foot path to see a doctor! The most fantastic part of this girl's story is that she has been living at Wagingombe, about 9 miles away by car, since January, the only European (meaning white) in the village! Usually the Peace Corps personnel are sent out in two's, but she chose to do this because it was recommended, by one of her fellow workers. She stated that it has been a rewarding experience. She has been teaching 6th, 7th, and 8th grades. She stated that the African children are very hard working. Of course they pay for school, and must take entrance exams, so a minority, only, is in school.

We took her home as much out of our own curiosity and astonishment as to save her a walking trip. She lives in a minute brick structure such as is lived in by the other African teachers. The school itself is made of brick and looks quite nice. She had two tiny rooms, and one for cooking.

Actually the kitchen is in a little room separate from the house, as in the other African houses. She didn't like to go alone outside, although it was in her own back court. She has no electricity, had a kerosene refrigerator, but didn't use it because she said it cost too much.

Actually, I think she wanted to live as the Africans do, and I think she has succeeded. She had nothing even remotely resembling a bathroom except for a small pan to wash in. She had an Asian type latrine, which is a hole in the ground. There are some mysteries surrounding this, which I haven't solved yet. Her term is up in September, and she plans to do a bit of traveling before she returns to Detroit. She has also been in a R. C. convent for five years, but decided it was not for her! I agree.

We later heard a rumor that the Peace Corps were American spies! But not this young woman.

The other day she walked 45 miles to Njombe in favor of the newest official Tanzanian policy, The Arusha Declaration, with her students, just to prove she could do it and to show she was in sympathy. There are around 400 Peace Corps workers here in the country, but she said they are being eased out. Many reasons I guess. We thoroughly enjoyed her company and plan to see her again September the 2nd. She visited Njombe every three weeks, someone came and got her, and that was the extent of her European association.

We will be in Nairobi for three months as Dave has no doubt informed you, and our address is on the envelope here if he hasn't told you.

Perhaps Dave is finally fulfilling his true ambition(s); he is preparing our *shamba* (cultivated field or garden) behind the house we will be living in on our return—it is on the hill facing the mountain. The other day he said he was going over to work on his farm??

A letter from Dorothy Harnish states they saw you at Spruce Lake. They bought a place, and perhaps told you about it, close to Doylestown.

We have been marvelously healthy. The children are playing in the sand in the best Creative Playthings manner, minus their expensive toys. The eggs come into the house still warm from the hens, and I think they are hoping to see an egg laid. Just poked up the fire for dinner (main meal) and must get busy.

Love,
Flo

Master Thomas Hershey (Hiram & Janie's son)

October 2, 1967
Nairobi, Kenya

Dear Tommy,

It is very easy to remember that you have a birthday soon, because, if you remember, our baby, Anne Elizabeth, was born on your birthday! Did you remember that? I wonder if you'll have a party? I am thinking of having a little party here for the children although Anne herself would probably be too little to know it's a party for her.

Do you know what we're doing now? Mommy and Daddy Harnish go to school! We are trying to learn how to talk Swahili—because that's what many of the Africans talk. We can't understand what they are saying unless we learn to speak like they do. To say "hello" in Swahili you say "*Jambo.*" To say "goodbye" you say, "*kwa héri.*" Now you know three words.

What do you think Marie, David and Anne do all day while we go to school? They go to the park where there are about a dozen or so other children and play! There are two African *aayahs* (babysitters) there to watch them. One of them is quite old and cannot speak English and the other one is young and speaks English well. The children call it "Playschool" and they like to go there. They have juice and cookies in the morning, and we eat sandwiches and fruit with them at noon. There is a crib for the baby to take her nap there under the trees, and the rest of us nap on a blanket in the grass. They have a swing, a "jungle-gym," a sand-box, and a small table and chairs. Our baby walks quite well now and likes to be with the other children.

Here we see a lot of things that are carved from wood. There is an old man who comes to where we go to school and brings things he has carved to sell—like elephants, rhinoceroses, giraffes, and other things we can see him carving right over there, and once we went and saw many families from one special tribe carving. Even boys help and they are very talented!

I'll bet it is getting warmer every day! We are looking forward to warm weather because it has been quite cool here—especially in the early morning and evening. Here the sun always comes up at 7 A.M. and goes down at 7 P.M.

I wonder how you like school this year. Do you learn lots of new things? Was it cold or warm at Cape Cod? Do you watch TV a lot now? Here in Nairobi there is TV, although they say it's on only in the evening.

Please give our love to Peter, Jimmy, and your Mommy and Daddy.

Love,
Aunt Flo and the other Harnishes
(Marie, David, Anne, and Dave)

November 12, 1967
Nairobi, Kenya

Dear Janie,

I was delighted to get your letter—I was wondering how everything was, and am wondering again—I hope you're not

One thing I found most interesting in language school: when I tried to think of a Kiswahili word I didn't know, the word came out as a Pennsylvania Dutch word which I learned in my bilingual family as a child. An Italian woman who was in language school at the same time as we were, said her words came out in "Italian." It must be that we have a language center in our brains.

going at too frantic a pace! As for me, life is not quite as easy here as it was in Ilembula. From the standpoint of a student—there's always something hanging over your head to be studied—but you're usually able to think of something else to do! Like writing this letter for instance. I've learned one thing—I may be getting old, but I'm still able to memorize (maybe not as much as I should!). Right now we have to learn the Lord's Prayer, The Apostles Creed (do you know it in English—we learned it in a Presbyterian Church in Philly), and a prayer—all in Swahili. Our final test will also test us on some of the chapters of Luke—as well as 5 minutes of conversation, which I am sure will seem interminable.

Our longest word to date was—*atakayewaungavisheni*. This word means "who is going to marry you" *i.e.,* the minister who will perform the ceremony. It is certainly most gratifying to learn this language—it's awfully frustrating too. The other day we listened to a tape of the news—well, we couldn't understand a word of it—a completely different vocabulary is used and of course they talk so fast! As anyone says who is learning a new language.

We have been going to the Nairobi Baptist Church since we are here. It is **most** stimulating. The minister is from Scotland. He stimulates your thinking very much. He really has a captive audience; it is composed of about 1/3rd African, about half European (any white person), and some Asians (Indian). The church is usually packed—modern structure not too large—Dave says about 300. Most of the Mennonites here go there. There are about 40-45 Mennonites here in and around Nairobi (including women and children!).

Don Jacobs (former) bishop of the Mennonite Church of Tanzania, and now sort of a director of the Mennonite work of East Africa lives close by. (He's Merle Jacobs' brother—well , you know him—he's Roma Ruth's brother!) He has been giving a series of lectures at this church every Tuesday and Thursday evening. He certainly is stimulating. We were at their place too last night, only a little ways from here. They just moved into a lovely home and we had a very good time. L. Weaver from the Goshen area, is here at the University of Nairobi for his junior year. He had his guitar along and sang some. There were mostly boys there and Marie is beginning to find out that sometimes girls aren't wanted—at that age anyway! She had a good time though I think. The baby is into absolutely everything now! She's really at a cute age though—just beginning to say a few sounds that might be words but we can't quite tell. The *aayas* insist she can say *mbya* (means "bad" or "naughty") a word which flows rather freely at the playground I fear!

Are you interested in any material or baskets or anything else from here? Nairobi is the place to get them. Just let me know.

There are several books I am interested in. How much of a discount did you say you can get through that place you send to? (I'll make no more paragraphs.)

My folks 50th wedding anniversary is today. They had open house. Dave is thinking of climbing Mt. Kilimanjaro in December (5 days), so the children and I may spend the time with my youngest brother, Ralph. He's here in Kenya about 4-5 hours away—have one child, a boy, age 18 months. Maybe I'll get to Ilembula the day after Christmas or so. We get *Time, Christian Living, Gospel Herald*. You may hear from someone here interested in nursing literature. I'm glad to hear you're going into nursing! Brubakers at 111 Elfreth's might be interested in opening their house to your concerts at Christ Church. I wish we were there to do it! So glad to hear about Louise. David stepped on a bee yesterday—today he skinned his knee—loves flowers and colors nicely and sings. Have you seen the Housmans?

Love, Flo

December 18, 1967
Limuru, Kenya

Dear Hirams,

We are here at the Limuru Baptist Center just outside of Nairobi about 30 minutes, at an altitude of 7,000 feet. It is beautiful here, and I have never seen more beautiful thick green grass anywhere. This is the annual TAP Retreat and we will be here for a week and 2 days. My brother Ralph, his wife Carol, and their 21-month-old son Randy are here, as well as Esther Clemens from your church whom we have finally met. One girl (married) looked so familiar. Here she's from my home church in Indiana and I haven't seen her since she was a child—how I've aged!

TAP Retreat at Limuru, Kenya. Harnish family standing third from left. Ralph and Carol Rheinheimer 7th from left.

We left the Mennonite Guest House yesterday and hated to go. Elizabeth Hostetter (Eastern Board) is certainly a good hostess and made our stay most pleasant. It was a privilege to study Swahili. We are not fluent but can carry on very elementary conversations— if we use it now at Ilembula we should become more fluent. (P.S. We both passed our tests—oral and written!)

Dave playing tennis in Nairobi (high elevation) in preparation for climbing Mt. Kilimanjaro. During language study.

Dave is going to climb Mt. Kilimanjaro next week, while the children and I go home with

Ralph's. He's not sure he'll make it, as many don't, so he's been playing a lot of tennis to toughen up. My brother Ralph didn't make it, once, and most of his group didn't. It is really a difficult feat. I have little desire to do it at this point. It is really just an endurance test!

This week we will be discussing a book by Dr. Kaunda, the President of Zambia, *A Humanist in Africa,* which I recommend to you highly. Dr. Paul Miller (Goshen) gave the sermon this morning and the main point was that the humanism as experienced in the Bible will ever exceed that inspired by man, *i.e.* man is like God. We are ever entertaining so many new ideas. I often wish I could share them with you, Janie, but by the time I sit down to write, the ideas have evaporated (or have been amalgamated) or seem too complicated or trivial to write. Right now in East Africa everything *Bantu* (African) is being eulogized—this being a reaction to colonialization.

This is now Thursday. I am a little frustrated about attending the meetings because of the children. Most of the couples do not have children so you really feel it if they make noise.

One of the new ideas we have gained is this—perhaps I should say insights—the African church tries to get a consensus of opinion and then seeks the "truth." The western church seeks the "truth" first then tries to get a consensus. The result is unity in the African church, which is the more to be desired?

It's Friday now! I must get this off. Other people that are here whom you might know are Jim and Lorraine Culp, Eric and Fran (Steiglitz) Schiller, Ron and

Anna Roth and Don Jacobs family in Nairobi.

Hershey Leaman family in Nairobi at the TAP Retreat.

Joyce Moyer, and maybe a few others. Don Jacobs has been giving some lectures again on *Bantu* Theology, which we heard him give in Nairobi last month—a series of 8 lectures. He is **so** stimulating! Hershey Leamans have left for the States yesterday and he will be in school for his Master's for at least a year—Pittsburgh I think. We are fine. The baby has a chest cold—had fever but is good now.

I do hope you have a **most** wonderful Christmas. We shall miss seeing you then.

Are you going to school in January?

Much Love,
Flo and the family

LETTERS

1968

February 5, 1968
Ilembula, Tanzania

Dear Janie,

We enjoy hearing from you so much. First I must tell you that the Christmas packages have arrived and you have never seen such delighted children! You couldn't have pleased them more, and they have been busily engaged in the many activities ever since. In fact I have been having trouble shooing them out of the house even on sunny days. The first package arrived January 24, and the others in the week and a half following. You must have remembered that I have an interest in crewel embroidery, and I am positively delighted with the pillow. I look forward to doing it. Dave is more than pleased with his Robert Frost book too (so am I!). Thank you for your very appropriate presents.

Please don't think that we are having so much leisure here right now! Sometimes I think I might as well be back in America! Right now, a plastic surgeon and his family from Texas are here for a few weeks and are eating all of their meals with us. They have two children, 4 and 5, so our children are very

Visiting local school at the time of Dr. and Mrs. Dave Herr's visit. Left, Mrs. Herr and two Herr children (from Texas); right Flo Harnish behind Anne, Marie and David Harnish. The children are holding school counting supplies. All are seated on three legged stools, carved from single piece of tree trunk.

Carol Rheinheimer with son Randy Rheinheimer in Kenya, while Dave Harnish climbed Mt. Kilimanjaro. (At Rheinheimer house).

happy to have someone to play with, although at times there are more quarrels than I think I can stand. I usually send them out then. The surgeon's name is Dave Herr, and he used to be from Lancaster (now a Presbyterian). He and Dave (Harnish) knew each other both at EMC and in Philadelphia in Med School, and I had met him before, too, in Philadelphia. Right now they are in Itete taking the German doctor and his family there (I shall miss them) because he is being transferred there. Then here we shall get a Dutch (Holland) couple to help at Ilembula. They seem very nice, but have no children since they have been married less than a year. They are both (I think I did say that) doctors, but don't know how much she will be involved in hospital clinical work. Perhaps she will do some teaching. Dave is teaching in the nursing school—did he tell you?

Right now, for a few minutes, all is quiet here. The children have gone over to the L_____ (Swedish and Swahili) for the first time to play. The language problem seems to create very little of a barrier if they once get over there.

We spent Christmas with my brother Ralph in Kenya while Dave climbed his mountain. We had a fine time, although we all had a 24-hour virus or something—one of the few illnesses we have had here. However, when we first got back here to Ilembula, the baby got an eye infection (fine now), the next week she got larva migrans—a small worm that crawls around under the skin (fine now), and now she has one of the blackest eyes you ever did see, from a fall.

The other time we were here, before Nairobi, they went barefoot all the day long, but now we must keep shoes on them, poor things. That was the dry season, and this the rainy. Generally speaking, we have been healthier here than at home, and I hope it lasts. I certainly remember some long runny-nosed winters anyway. How is it with you? We have had some rashes here and there, though none too serious.

You should see the profusion of flowers we have here. It is a horticulturist's heaven. You could do anything here with flowers and vegetables during this period of the year. We have planted a small vegetable garden, which is Dave and the children's project. It is wonderful to see them working together on this and they are having a wonderful education. Plus, we hope to have **many** (?) vegetables.

This is afternoon after naps now. David and Anne are still sleeping. Right now I would like to have a dryer! This is the rainy season, and you no sooner get your laundry out than it begins to rain—and I mean pour. I have everything inside now, hoping it will dry in the kitchen.

The children are enjoying that book of *Story Time Tales* very much, the Herr children too. But have you read the old children's stories lately? Gory!

I am wondering how much Dave told you about his successful climb up Mt. Kilimanjaro. It is at a height of 19,300 feet, one of the highest peaks in the world. One does not need picks, axes, or ropes, except for a walking stick, but after about 14,000 feet the oxygen content of the air lowers to such an extent that most people get altitude sickness. Dave couldn't eat for a day and a half. Towards the top he said everyone was just gasping for breath, their hearts were pounding, and they had to rest every two steps—literally! Some of the girls didn't make it after the third hut (the last one), but most of the others of a group of 12 (Mennonites) made it.

One of the boys admitted that it was the hardest thing he ever did, and the only thing that kept them from turning back was the mortification of telling that they hadn't made it. It was that same week that two other climbers died—they had gone up without guides. On Dave's group's way up, they met one of these coming down, feet first on a stretcher, if you know what I mean. As far as we know, the other one is still dangling from a rope in a position too hazardous to attempt a recovery of the body! Well, Dave is proud of himself. I am trying to understand the psychology of mountain climbing now. As for myself, I knew from the beginning that I'm too chicken!

I forgot to ask Dave if he had ever heard of a condition like Betsy I. has. He's not here now. Please give her (and him) our regards, as well as the Browns (both families), the Bookbinder (name escapes me just now—oh, yes, Eberhart), and the rest of our mutual friends that you see.

We're glad you liked the presents. There is just one thing, there was a separate (big) one for Hiram. It was mailed a bit later. Has it arrived?

This paragraph is in response to your letter. I'm reading your letter. Your talk about Christmas caroling made me a bit lonesome for Elfreth's Alley and caroling at Christmas. We did have a very nice Christmas at my brother's (except Dave—he was tired) but it was warm and a bit different. It was very much Christmas, but we weren't together. It is a Catholic place, and two of the Sisters (American) had us over for a very traditional Christmas dinner the night Dave got back. I'm so sorry to hear about Louise again. Any good news yet? I do not know if we can send mail to Nigeria. There was one letter waiting here for us from them last July when we first arrived, but I regret to say I have not yet answered. I shall send your greetings and your message when I get a letter written. Yes we did get your lovely Christmas card. Don't know about Esther—we saw her several times.

How is the Dave C. family? We heard their troubles have not ceased. Dave's Aunt Mary was with us for a few days in Nairobi, and she was the nurse in charge when the children had their tragedy, and she recalled the whole event with us. (By the way, have you seen the Housmans?) How was the concert at Old Christ's Church? **Too bad** we don't live in Elfreth's Alley! Have you ever mentioned anything to the Brubakers? They might be willing to lend you their house for receptions. And have you been to the Met in NY? Hope you got to.

Are you in school? Yes I read about the new method of childbirth in *Time* using air pressure. Let's get with it—it sounds great, in fact, fantastic. Maybe this is a complete new breakthrough. If all they claim is true, it certainly is!

As to what we need? Well, the most urgent is a big power lawnmower, so we can see if we are stepping on any snakes. (I hope you know I'm kidding!) We wish the mission would buy one, but everyone else seems to take the snake threat with equanimity. When we got back from Nairobi, of course our barrels were here, so at the moment all of our children's books seem quite new and delightful. We had brought a huge set of Tinker-toys, a Bolts and Nuts set, Lincoln Logs, and had a couple of other sets—well, when we opened the barrels, they had apparently dumped everything and we had a big bunch of sorting to do!!! Some things like pencils and brushes were broken; I had brought my last year's Christmas present from you, the nutmeg grinder, plus a little bag of nutmegs and there were nutmegs in each of the three barrels.

The thing that bothers me most, is every now and then I think of one of the children's books that is missing. At the moment I know of three that are missing of our good ones, but we did leave some at home, so unless I ask someone to check, I won't know if they are missing or not! I guess I started out to say if we needed anything. There is one book by John Holt called *How Children Learn* that I am interested in, **if** it's good, and doesn't cost too much. Do you think you could get it out of the library, and tell me what you think of it? Also, Hoertzel's *Cradles of Eminence* was recommended by Miriam Seiber Lind in her column, and it sounded so good. Have you read it? Also, if you have any magazines that you are finished with and haven't allocated to anyone else, I think they are very cheap to send by surface mail.

Feb. 1968, Valentine's Day—Back center: Marie Harnish; Front Center: Anne Harnish; Right: David Harnish; Second from right: Bahtlet; Left: visitors.

This is getting to be such an epistle. A word about the children yet. I am enjoying teaching Marie, mostly kindergarten things, but am wondering if I have the right to devote so much time to one child alone. I am also quite frustrated in allocating the time in my day's schedule. She loves it and does not hesitate to help me remember—in fact it is more like nagging! Sometimes I have David too, he colors, or listens to the story. Since the Herrs are here, sometimes he plays with them.

The baby is more of a problem. Sometimes I have to let Bahtletti take care of her, but she can't always do this with all the work she has to do here. The baby is certainly at a cute stage. She will be 16 months tomorrow, and I still think she looks more like Jimmie than our other two! I am beginning to think about the potty now. So far she likes to sit on it but doesn't know why. David is still our good singer. He sings every bit as well as Marie does, and I think he knows all the songs she does. We have our records and record player here, but unfortunately so far have not gotten a transformer, and so have not been able to play them.

So much for all that.

Much love,
Flo and family

P.S. Thank you for driver's license bit! (This ought to last a while!)

April 8, 1968
Ilembula, Tanzania

Dear Janie,

Usually after I unlock the door for our girl, Bahtletti, to get in at 6:30 A.M., I indulge myself and go back to sleep, but this morning my mind seems rather active already (you might think otherwise) so I decided to write to you. I reread your letters yesterday and was surprised to see that I hadn't heard from you since January. I don't know why I'm surprised though, the way we get mail around here. When we first came before we went to Nairobi, we got mail regularly, twice a week, but lately, during this rainy season, we are lucky if we get mail once a month.

Lorry and Landrover stuck in mud. Dr. Dave Herr to right of Landrover.

The roads are absolutely unbelievable they say. Last night some missionaries arrived from Dar es Salaam via the great (!) north road, and they said at one point there were 220 lorries (by actual count) waiting where a bridge had been washed out (on to a roundabout)—probably through some muddy field. They were able to dodge in, around, and through them because they had a small VW. I can't remember the last time the mail came in a regular way. It is completely hit or miss, with someone who goes to Iringa to get the mail, or Njombe, if we want to post anything. Normally, the mail comes in a post-bag on the bus from Iringa to Mbeya, if you have a map or are so inclined to look, but the buses have not been able to pass on the road. Sometimes the mail bag is not dropped off at our little village, and then we have to make a mighty effort to trace the mail bag. Mail is taken somewhat casually, you see, here. You could really get frustrated by this whole deal, but there is just no use. This year there has been much, much, rain, here, and that is the reason for all this trouble with the roads. Also, I haven't been off this place since we got here January 1, and I think I am getting a little stir-crazy.

When I first got up this morning it was dark. I lit a candle to type this, but now it is daylight. It does seem very cloudy and a little dreary, but here, within a space of 5 to 15 minutes, it changes from dark to light, or vice versa. Also, throughout the entire year, there is very little variation in the time of dusk and dawn. Seven A.M. and 7:00 P.M., a clean division of 12 hours. That has its advantages, but I miss the surprise and change of saying, "the days are getting longer now—or

shorter now." Weather-wise though, we really have very little kick coming. It is just ideal weather all the time. They say
after the rains stop in May, it will be cold, and then it will
be like when we first arrived—very crisp in the mornings
and evenings. But, if the sun comes out, which it usually
does because of no clouds and no rain, in the middle of the
day it is quite hot. I remember how shocked we were at the
chilliness. I was really misguided in what clothing to bring.
At times it is just perfect suit weather, but I left all of my
suits at 111 Elfreth's because we were told to bring "summer
clothes with sweaters." I have learned since that the people
to whom we wrote, are **very** frugal, and have only one or
two changes of clothing, and literally do as stated—summer clothes with sweaters. This is Dr. and Mrs. Stern, who
are at present in Germany, but who have been in various
parts of Africa all their lives. They do such things as keep
a basin of water to wash their hands in, so as not to waste
too much water. I think they have had to, because they
have had seven children, have educated them all, (she
taught them up to about grade five I think) and among
them there are doctors, teachers and I think preachers.
They have spent some years in South Africa, and to hear
Dr. Stern, you would think the situation between East and
West Germany is **far** worse than the situation in S. Africa.
Guess it's all right to say that in a letter. Let me know if
anything is deleted!

Just now the rain has come. (Still before everyone is up,
although Bahtletti is here in the kitchen.) Suddenly these
rains come. Sometimes we can see them approaching over
the plains, and then I run to get in my laundry—on Monday
and Thursday. How I need a dryer! (That will change in a few
weeks, though, then it will be perfect drying weather.) Usually the rain is very heavy, what we would call a cloudburst at
home, and it is very compelling. I often wonder what it must
be like to be in one of these mud huts with a grass roof. We
have a tin roof, and the rain thunders on it.

Marie, David and Anne Harnish being given a ride by Charles, garden worker.

Charles, a 15-year-old boy who helps us out, told me the other day that the heavy rains have damaged some of the mud huts around. After the rain is over, there are a few mud puddles around, but it seems to settle down into the earth very quickly. We can see the river from here a little bit, but when it rains heavily we can see it all along its length almost. We live sort of up on a hill, and the hospital is up further yet, and then the village beyond that.

April 12, 1968

Someone is going to Iringa to mail letters, so I will finish this, although there is much more I could say. I asked Dave if he was writing to you, thinking to send this along, but he said he has nothing to write. He said our mail has been so mixed up since February, that he doesn't know what to say.

Last night David developed a temperature and a headache. Also sore throat. With headaches, we always think of malaria of course. He seems a bit better today, but still has a little fever, and is just lying around. We also had some mysterious rashes that I think I talked about before, but I had it so badly that my face was all swollen up, and I was miserable for a couple of weeks. One possibility was the malaria medicine, although it is questionable, because the others have taken it again, and haven't particularly developed more rashes, but I have been afraid to take it. Malaria is really around this year because of the very heavy rains. In fact, about two weeks ago, the cook for one of the other missionary's oldest son, age six, died from it. Our house girl, Bahtletti, was also off for a few days with it.

Our biggest worry here, though, is still the snakes. It was most disheartening the other day to find a small green snake **inside** the house. We don't know how it got in, but it may have come in at the ceiling corners, because we know that shortly before we came here some snakes did come in that way. We have now sealed the ceiling with ordinary white hospital tape in the children's room (where it was found), but they have free access up there in the attic to the other rooms. Dave went up and **carefully** examined every corner and could see nothing. We also have scorpions in this area!

All this makes one wonder why one is here. For Dave it is quite clear-cut however. For me, I must find my own reasons. At the moment we are feeding three patients, two Africans and a doctor who was lost in the forest for several weeks, and barely survived. He is from New Zealand, and goes around to the mission hospitals to help out. We aren't sure if his condition is due to malnutrition (he did lose many pounds) or that it has been too much for him. I could write a whole two pages just about him, but won't. He is fascinating to listen to, but right now he has a **tremendous** need to talk, and I avoid him if I possibly can! I hope he publishes a book some day. We had heard about him from the missionaries at Shirati because he has been there.

Our Swahili is progressing, although slowly. The children can say very little, contrary to what many people have told us. Marie is progressing satisfactorily in school, David is enjoying himself, and Anne is as healthy and naughty as they come!

Love,
Flo

P.S. I highly recommend the book *Out of Africa* by Isak Dineson. I have it and enjoyed it.

June 10, 1968
Ilembula, Tanzania

Dear Janie,

We were absolutely delighted to get a box of books from you last Tuesday, June 4! There was real excitement around here. Nothing can please me more than to get books. I have already read *The Martyrs*. (Very well written, but a bit disturbing I must admit. What do you think?) I helped Marie read those little Wonder Books the first time through, and now she just loves to read them. They are really easy and so funny. They also love *The Cat's Meow*, (a little better than I do!). Do Tom and Peter like it? And the best book of all for them is *Charlotte's Web*. The only thing is we already have a copy, and just finished reading it about a month ago,

David, Anne and Marie Harnish reading books at Ilembula.

chapter by chapter. It just happened that Dave's cousin, Helen Ranck, a teacher in Somalia, was spending a few days with us. She has to go back to Somalia through Nairobi, so I thought better than to have two copies of the same book, I would send it up to the new Mennonite school, Rosslyn, at Nairobi. Was that right? Maybe I should have returned it. Does Peter read it for himself? I just love the book, and was so sorry we already had a copy. I probably would never have thought of it (to send it there), but they had sent two books with Helen, *Little House in the Big Woods* and *Little House on the Prairie* for me to read to Marie (I must return them). Actually, they are from the Mennonite Center there, courtesy of Mrs. Paul Miller, who is taking Elizabeth Hostetler's place while she is in the States. Are you lost through this big maze of explanations? Anyway we were delighted with these books, and Dave too. I told him you sent him the only kind of books he really reads—stock market stuff. We got your last letter on the same day.

I'll answer your first letter first. The children enjoyed the birthday cards very much. You asked whether we want *Christian Living* and *Time*. We get them. *Christian Living* is usually several months late (but still appreciated) and *Time* is one to three or four weeks late. Even if we don't get other mail, we don't complain **too** much when *Time* comes. It's really our only way of keeping up with current events except for your letters. Since our radio was stolen, we can't listen to the news at all. We did hear horrible news of the latest assassination of Robert Kennedy on the day it happened, as well as the death and funeral, albeit briefly, from Africans who work with Dave in the hospital. I dare say we were no more shocked than you were. We still can't quite believe that this thing has really happened, even though we have read some of the details in one of the Tanzanian papers. We have been really surprised that the people from these other countries that are represented here at Ilembula really follow our elections very closely. Whatever happens in America really hits the front pages here, especially race riots, and things like this Kennedy thing. Coming back to what I was saying, we also get *Gospel Herald*, and Dave gets some medical journals.

Tanzanian flags were flown at half-mast for Robert Kennedy's death. This was surprising to us.

We wrote to Nd and Edet—I think it was in February. So far we haven't gotten the letter back. You pronounce Tanzania like this: tan-zah-neé-uh. By the way, I think you said the Housmans were going to Algeria, but I think it's Ethiopia, isn't it? It will be hard for them, because I know how frustrating it is when you don't know the language.

In a way you're lucky to get the opinion of someone else to evaluate the school progress of Tom and Peter. In another way, I have always felt it is quite unfair to evaluate a student except against his own progress. I wonder sometimes how Marie is doing, and yet my rationalization is that I am able to do for her (if I am able) what teachers strive to do and cannot in the classroom, *i.e.*, give individual attention. What happened is this: We got the Calvert kindergarten and first grade materials. I also started to have Marie read the first book in the Bible Story series—"Look, look, See the star," etc. Well she went through that in a hurry, and then I decided to get out the first grade teacher's manual, and teach her properly. So I did that, and as a consequence, she is now in the third primer of their series, with one to go. She hated to do the exercises, but just wanted to read, so I just sort of let her do as she liked. But to my surprise, several days later she wasn't here when it was school time. She told me later that she ran away with Rangnar (Swedish boy her age—plays with him a lot, but can't talk to him) so she wouldn't have to have school. I decided it was time to give her a break! But still, for her before-nap stories (we **still** take naps—nearly everyone does here but Dave, but he just **says** he doesn't. I've caught him dozing in his office several times!), and before bedtime stories, she often does the reading.

Now what do you think of a system like that? The boarding school children just come back for their summer vacations too. I think we will let things rest too for a summer vacation, except as she wishes to continue reading. After all, in the States she would not even be in first grade yet. I am pleased to see that the Calvert course used the new math. Marie was not quite so keen on that—she knows very well what 25 is, but to say that 25 is 2 tens and 5 ones, well that is something else again. Cousin Helen Ranck is an elementary school teacher so I plied her with questions while she was here. Incidentally, personally, I think two hours of homework after school is an awful lot. Don't you? I don't think I ever did that as a child, but possibly I would be greatly improved if I had! The children speak very little Swahili yet.

I am having some difficulty in getting this typed because Anne insists on sitting in my lap. Yesterday she developed a fever with no other symptoms, and in the night it went up to 103. Today Dave looked in her throat, and it was just covered with big white spots—so he started penicillin, but that was only this noon. Her temperature is down now, but is she ever irritable. She can't swallow, so she just keeps her mouth full of saliva; every time her mouth opens a big pile of spit comes out! A week ago she had a little fever and a beginning cold, but seemed to be pretty well over that. We had gone to Bulongwa, a new hospital which has no doctor yet, so Dave went for a few days. On the road, there, we saw some of the prettiest scenery we have ever seen, bar none. It was cold there; they even have frost at times. And this is the tropics! Here it is chilly too—I put sweaters and hooded jackets on the children in the mornings.

It is now the next morning. With the aid of some aspirins and a little sleeping medicine, we all got a good night's sleep for a change. Anne got the sleeping medicine, not us. She had such a sore throat that she couldn't even eat or drink, and I had to choke the medicine down her throat. Poor thing. This morning she seems much better. Just a little fussy, not bad.

This is the third sheet. I hope these letters make up in quantity what they lack in frequency and quality!

Your letter about your long walk with the children sounded so wonderful. Here I have problems—in the first place, Anne won't walk! I have already tied her to my back as the Africans do, and that works fairly well. It's a little more comfortable than the carrier I have because it doesn't cut into the shoulders as much. As for the African women, having a child doesn't stop them from going in the least. Most women in the child-bearing age have a child strapped to the back when they are walking about. And then, the paths we would walk on are composed mostly of dust (the rains have stopped), which doesn't bother walking so much, but when you know all the diseases and parasites that are here, you wonder. Actually, it doesn't bother us too much.

But then the other thing is, there are so many snakes around. We wouldn't dream of walking in tall grass! However, I distinctly recall Dr. and Mrs. Stern and their college-age son coming up from a walk from the river past our house through grass as high as their heads. In this house we saw our 4th little green poisonous snake this past Saturday. And guess where I found it. On top of the shelves, inside the lamp, where the children's toys are. This one was dead. The light had apparently been too hot for it. Now the question arises: "How long was it there, and where did it get into the house?" We are at the moment having a workman seal up the cracks from where we thought they were coming down from the attic. The ceilings are fiberboard, and there are a lot of cracks at the edges of the walls. I had sealed this room (the children's room where they seemed to be coming from) with tape from the hospital, but there was still a small space where I suppose it could have come from. That's why I would like to know how long it was there. The other three were very much alive, and I must confess that I have an absolute horror of stepping on one of them unwittingly, or worse, one of the children.

This snake business is my worst problem here. This doesn't bother other people as much as it does me! But what's to be done? I don't know. But I do think the least we can have here is a snake-proof house. It's one thing when they come in if you leave the door open, but quite another when they come from within the house. Then you don't feel safe anywhere. None of the other houses here have had this problem, just this one, and we have discovered that it is noted for it. We heard that once a large lizard (must have been a good yard and a half long) came up out of the toilet. That was several years ago. I must admit I turn lights on at night, and leave a light on for fear of stepping on one of these despicable objects. To terminate the subject of snakes—a big one, about 5 ft., also a very poisonous tree climber (ours are probably the children of this type) was seen by Dave about three weeks ago, in the middle of our storeroom where we keep our chicken food, assorted boxes and stuff. On either side of this room there is a room for laundering, and a room for wood. Well, Dave hit the snake with something but it got away, and climbed the big thorn tree just outside our house. For several hours, the boy that works for us and the workman here, were trying to get it. When Dave came back from the hospital it was still there, so he went and got a man with a gun to shoot it. Which he did, with one shot, and for about $1.40. That night, David had a terrible night! He was so restless, and was crying, and talking about snakes and fangs. It was just too much for him.

The funny thing about the children, though, we tell them not to go in the weeds and flowers because of the snakes, and before you know it they're in there again, even though they seem to be afraid when you talk to them. The funny thing about the Swedish children—they run barefoot all the time, through the grass, etc. Actually, considering the number of snakes in the area, very few people are bitten. Far, far fewer than are killed in the States by cars every day. And thus I console myself. At night we crawl into our mosquito-netted beds with great pleasure, I can assure you.

The mosquito nets were not for the mosquitos—there was not a lot of malaria in the southern highlands where we were located. They were for those green snakes, which we knew could climb. I tucked them around the children very carefully when they went to bed at night. When we got back state-side, I did not let the children ride with anyone else in a car for a long time, because of the car death statistics that I had hammered into my brain (more people in the U.S. are killed by cars, than by snakes in Tanzania). Also, it took both Dave and me years, before we could reach into greenery (such as pachysandra) without looking for snakes.

I wonder how Jimmy is. He certainly seemed very mature. As for David, I don't know if I imagine it or not, but in many ways he seems far less mature than Marie was at this age. I don't mean in things like counting, coloring, singing, etc.; but like crying when he falls, and sitting still in church (he is absolutely the worst squirmer I have ever encountered), etc. He is still quite large for his age (actually, Anne is the same height and weight as he was at her age—do you think she'll be tall?), tall and slender, with a large head. Some of his intellectual accomplishments are good, singing ability above average, and in one memory game we have, he often beats us, although we really try. (It's a game called *Pairs*, and our whole family plays, and David particularly just loves it.) It may well be that that this is the only difference between girls and boys. He really needs other boys to play with now I think. One thing I noticed in the children's play; when they are making roads (David was doing it yesterday, that's why I think of it now), instead of making nice bridges for their trucks and cars to go over water and gullies, they just throw in stones until the vehicle can pass. That's what they learn in Africa! The children are always talking about "way back in America" we did this or that. Nearly a year now.

The hospital here has I think 200 beds (in response to your question). There is a Holland doctor here also, and his wife is an M.D. as well, but only does a little work in the hospital. They have been married about a year and a half and I think are hoping for children, so she didn't want to tie herself down too much in the hospital. There is a nursing school here, I think around 50 students or so, and it is a good one. It is relatively new. Right now they are being forced by the government to add a fourth year of mid-wifery to their usual three-year program. Isn't that just one of the smartest things a country like this can do? In conjunction with that, they must expand the maternity unit here at the hospital, and to get funds for this is a problem. It is a Lutheran school and hospital, so funds will probably have to come from the church. The government has given no money, just says this must be done. The nursing school at present has two Swedish instructors—one the director—and an African instructor. Here the nurses are classified in some way

Above: Nursing students, pastor on left, Swedish missionary instructor in center. March, 1968. Left: Nursing student on trip to local village with hospital Landrover.

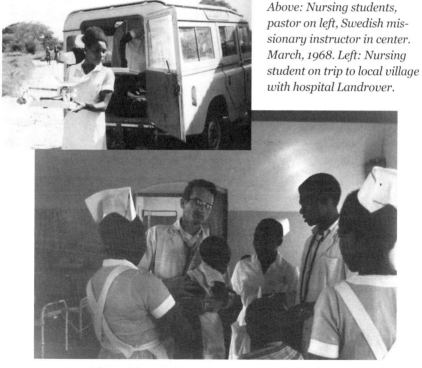

Dr. Harnish (2nd from left) and [local doctor] Dr. Kadeta (2nd from right), along with nursing students, examining patients.

I don't understand fully, but a Grade A nurse corresponds to what we have in the States—a three year R.N. Then they have many other gradations, and get government grants to the hospital according to how many and which type are employed. They also have "dressers" which are something like nurses, too, but usually have a little more training than their Grade B nurses—don't know how it compares to Grade A. Dave also gives lectures in the nursing school, and I heard he gives a good lecture!

You wanted to know if we are in the bush. Yes, I would say that we definitely are. Here in the village of Ilembula, we have maybe three stores that sell things like pieces of cloth, flashlights, candy, bicycle wheels, local rock salt, and miscellaneous items. They are often one room only, and are typical of East African countries. Many items are made in China. And cloth I think comes chiefly from India. Many

people talk of living in the "village." I am really not too sure what they mean, because you have fields between nearly all of the houses. I am not too sure about this, but I think often several families live in one

Typical house, man at left unidentified.

Thatched roof house 50 yds from our house. In 1969, house was torn down.

Local Ilembulan house – unknown persons walking.

A village scene near Ilembula.

house. Most of the houses are made of mud with thatched roofs, but here and there you see tin roofs—as we have on our house. The houses are often arranged around a central court, with the cooking done over three stones set in the ground, inside though. When you get into one of these little courts and get over your feeling of strangeness, you see what a really neat arrangement it is. The floors are of dirt, but they have become so hard that they are almost like cement, and are swept just as ours are.

To get our groceries, we go one of two places. One is Njombe, which is about an hour and a half away in good (dry) weather and anything above that in rainy weather. The roads then are just impossible. In this country you must have either a LandRover (David is currently enchanted with LandRovers, and calls his tricycle a LandRover) or a VW, such as we have. There are advantages to either, and I hear Dave discussing the virtues of one or the other frequently. We live about seven miles off the main road through Tanzania (the Great North Road), but if you'd see it it's not so great. We heard that there is surveying going on for a new road, also a railroad is to go through here close by.

Did you read in *Time* about the pipeline to Zambia? We had some of their patients flown here by helicopter. That was some excitement here—the first helicopter in this area ever. We joined the crowd that was around the helicopter—the children and I, that is, Dave had to take care of the patient. The pilot was sitting in his all-glass enclosed front, trying to read a book, but every so often he had to shoo the crowd back. I wish I could describe the scene to you. It was really very funny, and I felt sort of sorry for him. He must have felt like a monkey in a cage. I started to say about the pipeline. Marie and David have laid quite a few pipelines in their sand now. Just now they wanted me to come and see their road. They have some mountains, slippery mud, rivers, bridges, etc., on their way from Dar es Salaam to Iringa to Bulongwa. We have done **nothing** with our recorders since we left Nairobi! Shame.

Next day now—Wednesday. I suppose if you write an epistle like this you can't expect to finish it in one day. Anne seems much better this morning, but Marie threw up all of her dinner last evening. She seems okay today though. Maybe she just ate too much fresh bread and jam yesterday (didn't we all?). I made some jam from a fruit called *matunda damu* which means, "blood fruit!" It turns red when you cook it or just cut it. The jam turned out fairly well, nice and red, with one of those funny, unidentifiable tastes.

You wanted to know something of our surroundings and what Iringa is like. It's 140 miles to Iringa, and that is where we get the bulk of our groceries. It's 4 to 5 hours each way. We really buy in bulk, too! 200 lbs. of sugar, 12 5-lb. bags of flour, toilet paper in a great huge box. We have been to Iringa one time since we got here in January! Other times we have either sent our order with someone else, or else have gotten things in Njombe, which is a much smaller place. Njombe has one "city block" of *ducas* which includes several petrol stations, and two groceries (with staples only, but some things like carrots and apples)—they grow not too far away which surprises us. They also have peaches and plums, and sometimes things like white grapes.

In Iringa you have a large market where you can buy many things like vegetables, fruits, coconuts, fresh produce, and rows and rows of cloth. Some of the cloth is very good quality, but some is just filled with sizing. The kind that is filled with sizing is very colorful, and is the kind the African women wear. They usually wear one piece, plus a cloth of some other kind to hold the babies on. Often they cover their babies with a second cloth to keep out the flies, dust, rain, etc. Although the babies don't wear too much in the way of clothing, they lie close to the mother's back and must be quite warm. In Iringa you have several streets of *ducas* that have materials, flashlights, teapots, etc. I have never fully satisfied my urge to visit them because usually I have children along (all ours!). I think you would really like to visit these shops, and also places like Dar es Salaam. I really think you should visit us, don't you? How about coming over and touring Europe with us on the way home? Just got that idea yesterday. We would also need a babysitter, **of course**.

Nairobi seems to be the hub of Mennonites here in East Africa, and some people think it's the end of nowhere to come here to see us. Maybe it is (by the map) but to us, it's home. We like it here, except for a few minor things we would change if we could, as I have mentioned before in this letter. The scenery is beautiful, I look out of our west windows (children's room, living room, dining room) first thing in the morning, (it never looks the same) and last thing at night, and here we see the most glorious sunsets. You look out over the plains, which are dotted with houses (African), fields, sometimes herds of cows can be seen, trees here and there, and then in the distance you can see this range of mountains that is ever-changing. To the other sides you can see part of the mission complex here. I will try to draw a little sketch of the mission here.

I have come to the 7th, and I hope last, page. I had some kind of peanut-type vegetable, tiny potatoes in their skin—

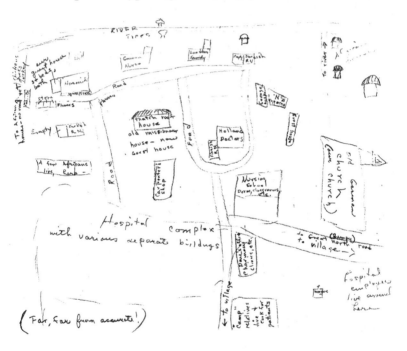

how I hate to peel them, but that's how they grow here—and plain cooked meat fresh from the cow. For dessert we had a rice custard. We usually eat our heavy meal at noon, which really makes a lot more sense. Our meat we buy at the door, about 17 cents a pound. You get big hunks of good red meat, hardly any fat, but very tough. If you get no bones it is called "steak." Once I got some kind of organ—it must have been a kidney. I often grind it. I sure do hate to handle that raw meat—because the inspection system is practically nil, although I understand they do have one. Now and then

Bahtlet preparing a Kuku (chicken) being watched on back porch by Anne, David, and Marie.

we also buy a chicken which Bahtletti butchers for us. We have also had rabbit, and sometimes tuna from a can. Last week we had a real treat—sausage that Dave had gotten in Njombe.

There are other things I could say, but I think perhaps it's not wise in a letter. The people here are really lovely. The Dutch doctor's wife and I are thinking of starting some sewing classes—is there such a thing as a pattern for a brassiere? All sizes. If there is, let me know, and maybe I will want to get some. There is another German wife who may have one.

What is Charles and Louise's address? How are they?

We have cats around here; perhaps *The Cat's Meow* is more appropriate than I have said, because we had a family of kittens born here, which are

Anne Harnish with kitten.

now half-grown. We are keeping one of them. The children have enjoyed this immensely.

You are more than welcome to use **any** of the books we left at home—nursing, medical, children's, other. Please feel free. Now, while I am talking about that—sometime when you are up there rummaging around on our third floor, will you dig deep down in the cedar chest (right-hand side I think) for my credentials and have them photo-statted for me? Tell me how much this costs. Also, check my files in the upstairs hallway—but excuse the mess. Seems like we can't be done asking for favors! I may be helping out a little in the nursing school here, and they want my credentials. It would be diplomas for High School, Goshen College, and University of Pennsylvania. That's all, I hope. I have my run-out R.N.'s license here. Speaking of books you might use—sometimes some of Dave's medical books on Microbiology and Anatomy and Physiology were far more helpful than the nursing texts—which tend to be too all-inclusive and therefore too brief. For Anatomy and Physiology, I particularly recommend one called *Dynamic Anatomy and Physiology*, but off hand I can't remember who the three authors are. There is a newer edition that I don't have, but if you take the course you might want to get it from the library, and consider buying it. Kimber-Gray-Stackpole-Leavell aren't so hot to my way of thinking, unless the new edition with which I am not too familiar is good. Maybe I just knew Leavell too well at Penn! What a shame that I am not there to be embarrassed by your questions. But I did some private tutoring—$5.00/hour!

There was something else I wanted to say but can't remember, so I'll quickly put this in the envelope before I do. David had a positive malaria slide last week, but certainly recovered quickly. Today (Thursday) Anne is fine. I'm fine; Marie's fine; Dave's tired. Oh yes, you asked me about entertainment—absolutely nil. Unless you count the films we saw last night from Shell Company! First time, but we did all enjoy them. What can I send you from here? Please tell me if there's something you want.

Love, Flo

July 15, 1968
Ilembula, Tanzania

Dear Janie,

We received with great pleasure both your last letter and a parcel of magazines last Tuesday! You should have seen the children and me fighting over the magazines—it was a regular tug of war. They wanted them all, and so did I! It really gave me a boost to have something to read, because I think I did tell you, that's what I miss most here. Both Dave and I don't complain too much if we get *Time* on time, even if we don't get too many personal letters. Often it's late, or like last week, we got three issues in one week! Thank you, thank you.

Now what better way to get a prompt answer back than to ask us what we want for Christmas! I went out to the children to ask them what they'd like, and they got real bashful and pleased, and both of them said, "I don't care what they send us." But I've noticed they keep asking me how long it is until Christmas! One thing about Christmas, we will not be able to spend it here at Ilembula. When I first heard it I was sick, but I have somewhat faced it now. Last year we were with my brother, Ralph, and Dave was on Mt. Kilimanjaro. We may be able to go there again, to Ralph's, or perhaps (and probably) to Aunt Mary's place at Shirati. You see, our annual TAP retreat will be at Nairobi again from December 14th to 23rd. From here to Nairobi it's a three-day trip really pushing it, and in four days it is also an ordeal. I do so like to get things ready, and think about it, and make things with the children, but TAP retreat is something we would not want to miss, for last year it was most inspiring. We may combine our vacation with it, since we need to go so far. Vacation in December!

Now, suggestions:

Anne—doll, take-apart pull toy, tea set.

David—boat, train, helicopter, or etc.

Marie—game, very simple sewing kit, doll (long comb-able hair, or etc!)

Dave—can't think what he wants. He just now said a book on African snakes, butterflies, insects, animals, or something of this type–East Africa.

Me?—Haim Ginott's book: *Between Parent & Child* (Christian Living, May 68, p. 33). I did read it just before I left the States, and liked it very much, but all the Philadelphia stores were sold out at the time, and I was not able to get it, along with the Holt book. Also—if you would find a sweater to knit, not too expensive, I'd love that.

None of these things are given in order of preference, and please don't strain your budget, but frankly we look forward to it. Am I learning to receive, or just getting greedy?

We have had a bit of excitement here lately. Last Saturday we heard a very strange call, repeated many times, from seemingly many places. Everyone was very excited, and our Charles (I sent his picture) thought maybe someone was caught by a wild animal—such as a lion. (Two years ago in this area and visible from the house, several women were killed by a stray elephant, although we have yet to see an elephant in Africa.) Anyway, we could see a lot of people running. They crossed the river, and we could see them way up on the hill on the other side of the river, and they seemed to be in white.

Well, it seems like a patient had stabbed two other patients and then taken off, with hospital personnel in full chase, giving their distress signal for help as they went. (So glad he didn't have a gun, and that it happened in daytime.) They caught him and we saw them bring him back. He had also made an attempt to stab himself, so his short white hospital coat was all stained with blood. What a sight, and what a crowd, and what a lot of questions we had to answer to the children! It will be a police case, but he was probably sick, since to our knowledge no robbery was involved. The patients are recovering satisfactorily after emergency treatment by the **DOCTORS**. It seems, that if you are in trouble, you give this piercing cry (our "help," but much more penetrating—I can still hear it), and people will drop everything and come to the rescue.

Charles has been asking if he could write to someone in America, so I gave him your address. Could you give it to someone, in his teens, who is not too disillusioned with life? You may already have received it. He has great dreams, but. There is an older boy who also speaks English to a certain extent who would like a "pen-pal" in the States. He's about 20. They have such a great curiosity about things in the States. Charles, the other day, was astounded that nearly every house has piped-in water, and the women don't carry it on their heads. I told him I tried it already, but it just falls off. The women here have very excellent, stately posture, and move with grace.

I must get this in this week's mail. Don't worry, I won't send 7 pages often. It costs too much to send! Glad you had the stamina to read it!

Much love, Flo

P.S. Please airmail those patterns I asked you for. Also any useful ones and maybe a simple shirt waist dress. I have started sewing classes, maybe a simple hooded jacket.

Master Peter Hershey (Hiram & Janie's son)

August 23, 1968
Dar es Salaam, Tanzania

Dear Peter,

Ever since your birthday early this month I have been wanting to write to you. I can still remember what a sweet, dark-
haired baby you were, and how proud your mother and
daddy were of you!

Right now we are in Dar es Salaam (the capital of Tanzania), staying with some friends. Dave is attending a Tanzanian Christian Medical Association meeting, while the rest
of us are here. Our friends are in TAP (teachers), the same
program we are. Your mommy might remember Francis
Steiglitz (Liz's sister)—she is married now to Eric Schiller
and they are the ones we are staying with.

Here we see many Muslims—the women wear black shawls—
and many Indians (here they are called "Asians," and are
often shopkeepers). We took three days to get here from
Ilembula, although we can make it in two, over very dusty,
bumpy roads.

The other night we had a meeting in one of the Catholic churches here, where the wives of the doctors went,
too. Do you know who is the President of Tanzania? It
is Julius Nyerre, and he was at this meeting, too, so we
got to shake his hand. We heard him speak a little (to the
people at the party), and we were quite impressed both
with what he was saying about Socialism in Tanzania,
and his very humble way of speaking.

Have you had a good summer? Did you enjoy Cape Cod? Do you remember the time we went there with you? We have pictures of you on that vacation. On the way here we stopped at a Game Park, and wanted to sleep in their tents and see their animals. Their tents were full (kerosene lantern is the only light at night—you'd love it), but we did see many animals, including our first elephants. Also many giraffes, which are

On safari. Roman Catholic church which we deemed large for the area. Dave standing in foreground.

so beautiful, zebras, buffalo, killbuck, but unfortunately no lions! We also had to sleep in the car—just no other place to sleep! Do write if you want to.

Love,
The Harnishes

P.S. Please tell mommy I got the patterns she sent and have already used some. I am so happy for them, as are the ladies.

September 11, 1968
Ilembula, Tanzania

Dear Janie,

I wanted to write to you from Dar, but that week flew so quickly. Then last week I was surely going to write, but Marie has been running a mysterious temperature off and on since the 18th of August, and last week it was between 103 and 104 (under her arm) for several days on end unless knocked down by aspirin. I didn't sleep well at all for several days, not so much because she was restless (a little), but I was just plain down worried. We don't know what was wrong with her, and she had absolutely no other complaints, and Dave couldn't find a thing. Blood tests (the ones you can get here!) were nearly normal, but Dave was saying something about infectious mono—don't know though. For the last three days (since Monday) she has been temperature-free, and I am so relieved. Please pray that I don't get so frantic, Janie! I just don't seem to put enough trust in God, although at times like this, you realize that if you didn't believe in God you don't know what you'd do. I do wonder if I'd have the stamina to release one of these little ones back to him! How do these African mothers bear it, who lose so many? It is easy to say that they are used to it, but personally I think it is a shallow, superficial remark, and that they feel it as keenly as you or I. Perhaps more so, having known the truth about real sorrow.

Here is a question for you: If all around you (but the missionaries) were carrying all of their water from the river, anywhere from 1/2 to 3 miles on their heads, would you water your lawn with your hose? Also, would you wash your hands every day?

I am quite overwhelmed with your generous gifts, and must confess that I **can't wait** until I get those books and the other things. I did not know that you were sending all those that I had mentioned. The one I really wanted very badly was the Holt, and I am very pleased that in your opinion he is good. I also wanted Ginott's book (I did read this rather hastily once) but am disappointed in *How to Raise Children in Your Spare Time*. I couldn't get it in the main library in Philadelphia before I left and it was all sold out in the bookstores, so

I really didn't know what it was like. Had only heard about it from a friend and the author on the radio. You have ordered *Cradles of Eminence* . . . too—I'm usually a bit more cagey— I try to read someone else's copy before I buy. However, I heard about this by reading M. S. Lind's "On the Corner" in *Christian Living*.

How lucky you are to have a whole week in which to **read**! When I hear of these single girls here who come back from vacation, I positively envy them. They'd never believe it, of course. But you know how vacations with small children are—especially here, where you trust **no one** but yourself for food, etc. I don't know how our projected vacation will be in December, because Dave wants to travel, I think. Your week at Music Camp sounded great, in all of its aspects. Also, I received another packet of magazines, and am delighted! They cost a bit more to send than I thought they would. Thank you. We also received a post office notice of a package for Anne. I shudder to think that you went ahead and sent that toy airmail! At her age, it probably wouldn't have mattered when it arrived. Perhaps someone else sent a package.

I am continuing with my sewing class. I am a bit frustrated because there could be about 5 of me teaching, and it wouldn't be too many! One lovely young girl has already sewn herself a shift from one of your patterns, and another older lady (the president of the organization) wants to make a shirtwaist. Frankly, she ought to have a brassiere first, but perhaps I can leave out some darts in the pattern! She said that was for younger girls when I showed her the pattern of the brassiere and seemed quite surprised. I don't know though, she may want one. I wish, of all the experiences I am having here, that I could share this one with you, since you are an expert in the field.

My **biggest** problem is the fact that we sit on mats on the floor, and of course the Tanzanians are quite comfortable sitting that way for hours, but for me it is absolute agony. I never could sit on the ground, even in America. This last time I begged for a table (they laughed at me and are quite astonished at my difficulty), and so, they went to the front of the church and got me a little table—I would say it's about two feet by three feet—and then I could work better. We meet in the church lobby. I'm planning to get some material from MCC I wouldn't mind having them meet here in the house, but it does have its problems (no diapers on the children for one thing), but sometimes I have them come on an individual basis. Of course they do everything by hand with needle and thread and some do a fine job nevertheless. They have far more patience than I. At the moment two women are sewing shirts for their boys, about a size one, which I had to cut the pattern of (grammar!) from another shirt. A couple of them finished shirts like that and said they were nice, but I myself haven't seen a finished one. Here, many men wear Mao-type shirts (collar-less) and I think I shall try that pattern. The president himself (Nyerre) wears that type. I am beginning to like them.

Here, by the way, one can buy many things made in China. In one of last week's newspapers out of Dar (English) there was a front-page article hotly denying collusion between the U.S. and U.S.S.R. before the Czechoslovakian invasion (being denied by the Russians).

Marie Harnish (left), David Harnish (right), Anne Harnish (2nd from right), playing in a pile of dirt near our house with Swedish missionary children.

Anne loves best playing in the mud these days, speaks mostly English, a little Swahili, and now and then a Swedish word— if I'm lucky enough to recognize it. David rides our English-built bike a lot, and we also have finally gotten a transformer in

Dar for the record player that we brought along, and he is absolutely enchanted with that. They have been over a year without it, and now he is old enough to manipulate it himself. It doesn't play at quite the right speed, but it's pretty good. Thank you for your very good letters with all the news. Write again soon.

What is the Hogge's new address?

Love,
F and the other H's

October 13, 1968
Ilembula, Tanzania

Dear Janie,

I stayed up last night until midnight crying and reading *Mrs. Mike*. It's really a terrific book, and I'm afraid I identified with her too much. (That's all I can think about today.) Did I see it on the best reading list in *Time* for a while? If I could only tell you how much I enjoy the magazines and books you have sent me! This last group came week before last—also has in it *Karen,* and two others as well as the magazines and children's magazines. They love those pictures where you have to find things in the trees and such, "hidden puzzles," I think it's called. We are truly grateful. Also thank you for that toy for Anne (it **was** from you!)—she loves it! (So does David.) It's an excellent vehicle for water and sand, which we have in abundance, and which she loves. We had a birthday party for her—the usual crowd came that comes every day (!) and the parents and other missionaries came for tea. Actually, Dave and quite a few of the others were gone last Sunday.

Anne's birthday party while Dr. and Mrs. David Herr were visiting Ilembula. Rear row of children: David Harnish, two Herr children.

Anne is a little mischief now. When she's alone she's fairly predictable, but when Esther L----- comes, which is nearly every day, you had better be on your toes. Last week one day while I was teaching Marie, they got into the bathroom and stuffed a large towel in the toilet bowl, a whistle, and a piece of cloth. Fortunately their little brains didn't think to flush it, or I don't know what would have happened! There was water all over the floor (not at all unusual), sand in the bathtub, and both had taken off their panties and at least one had gone potty (hope it was mine), and their panties were in the wastebasket, wringing wet. I decided then and there that Esther could not play here anymore during the period of time that I am teaching Marie. It's impossible! Esther is really a very sweet, good-natured child, but it's just when they're together. Anne is not toilet trained yet, although **some** days I think she's making progress. **Our** third was certainly not the fastest in this respect at least. Despite this paragraph, she is really at that very cute, innocent stage, and couldn't be improved upon. I must say, she drinks a lot of unboiled water, and unwashed food that we wouldn't dream of doing.

Some days now, I am having a bit of difficulty getting Marie interested in school. She's really something of a dawdler—or is that word taboo these days? Some days David comes to "school" too, and does some of the kinder-garten work that we didn't get done last year. That really distracts her. I don't know what she'd do in a whole room full of children! As for David, he breezes through whatever I give him to do. He has been working on some things with similarities and differences, which he recognizes immedi-ately, although now and then I am absolutely astounded at what they call differences! If there is the smallest dot on one picture that is not on the other, they say it is different. Usually these are printing errors, and they are meant to be the same!

David needs a lot of muscle coordination yet, especially with things like coloring. He takes his crayon, and with big, sweeping motions the whole picture is colored, in a matter of seconds! However, in cutting he works slowly and delib-erately. Marie is the exact opposite—she works slowly and meticulously. Part of this is due to age, I'm sure.

We usually have Sunday School on Sunday mornings before we walk up the hill to church. Miriam Housman had given us a lot of Sunday School materials that someone had given her that she didn't need. Some of this is very good. What kinds of things are your children doing in Sunday School these days? Think-ing of your church—what is the status of your building project? Do you ever get in to Diamond Street? Do you hear from John Ruths? The Browns—how are they? I haven't heard from Lou-ise for an age. Wonder how she is. How's Hiram's real estate business these days? Are there still places for sale? (In the little corner of my mind that I have for these things—it seems that everything was all sold years ago!) What is your reaction to the quilt sales being discussed in the G.H.? My mother just wrote about a very successful one they had in northern Indiana, and she was very proud of her contributions to it. How are your parents? Hiram's parents? Please give them both our greetings. Do you hear from Betsy or Winifred?

We are in the process of packing a few things to send you—from the shape of things, I think there will be two packages, also some things for the Kirchners in Philadelphia.

I hope to get them off this week—probably not 'til the Wednesday post. Probably I will get a letter from you in the mail, then I'll wish I had waited. We send post Monday and Tuesday, and get (if we're lucky) on Tuesday and Thursday.

Love, Flo

October 30, 1968
Ilembula, Tanzania

Dear Janie,

I must say I feel like I am writing to you so often you will soon be bored! I don't know how much time I'll have this evening, so I'll come right to the point. I would like to ask a personal favor of you—of course it involves money and time (not too much I hope)—and it is this: One of the German missionary wives whom we know fairly well has just had her third child, and is really in need of help from that booklet put out by the La Leche League: *The Womanly Art of Breastfeeding*, and I've promised to send it to her (through you of course!) but hated to ask **you** after I promised her. The day before yesterday she was here to see a doctor about the baby (now two months old) because the baby was crying a lot and wouldn't nurse well. (Soon they will no doubt put it on the bottle!) Her other children are three and one, and that in itself tells part of the story. Njombe is too far for me to see her and the doctor who sees her here is Dutch, has been married one and a half years with no children—in my opinion she needs a little more household help, more sleep at night, and the advice of another nursing mother! I wonder if you would be able to airmail her a copy—I really want to pay for this, but would you be able to wait until we get home? I have regretted many times that I did not bring my own copy, in which case I would loan it out. Are you finished in our attic at 111 Elfreth's? Did you run across my copy or are you going back? I'd like very much to have a copy of the book—by regular mail—I really need it. Maybe it's not too heavy so that airmail to her will not be too much, but she really needs help, **now**. Her address is: Mrs. Vladimar F., P.O. Box, Njombe, Tanzania, East Africa.

The packages (there are three now due to postal regulations!) which we sent you have come back! We will not be able to mail them now until November the 5th, when we will be going to Mbeya. I'm awfully afraid now that they won't get there before Christmas, and I'm really sorry. I will send you a list of contents and what is in each package, but not in this letter.

Today, I think, is Halloween—or is it tomorrow? I really can't quite remember, but we are going trick-or-treating at a few of the missionaries' homes here! Strictly American! I must say, this business of witches and spirits gives one pause here in this country where these beliefs are still so rampant! I've been reading some of the African Writer's Series in paperback and they are really educational.

Your schedule sounds absolutely impossible. I could never stand a schedule of that intensity for a very long time. I have moments of it here—especially since Marie and I started school again. However, you sound like you are doing fascinating and worthwhile things.

Your news, undisclosable, is wonderful! We enjoyed the pictures very much. Nobody has changed much in appearance except in size—the children, that is. Hiram's beard is very becoming. I've been trying to convince Dave he should have a beard, but no go.

Must go now.
Much love,
Flo

December 19, 1968
Limuru, Kenya

Dear Friends,

If this letter gets to you by Christmas it will be a minor miracle, but I hope it does. We are at the TAP retreat again here, just north of Nairobi. We stay here for about 8 days, and I must say it is one of the more stimulating conferences I have ever attended. We are talking about the "culture clash"— Africans and Americans, and how to "shake Jesus loose from culture." (Don Jacob's term.) He is certainly a man able to crystallize thinking. Anna Ruth Jacobs is helping with babysitting and so I too am having a very good conference. The grounds here are as lovely as any you would be able to find in the Poconos. Marie has found a friend her age (Cheryl Detweiler from Ohio) and is really having the time of her life. David is tagging along with them and enjoying it as well, although he had fever and a headache for a couple of days this week and is really not quite his usual self. It is probably a reoccurrence of malaria. Anne is happy too. There are many children her age here. This noon she cried to stay with Mrs. Jacobs, rather than come to me!

Dave, Flo, Anne Harnish, lower right. Marie and David Harnish, 7th and 8th from right in front row. Teacher's Abroad Program, Limuru, Kenya. A Mennonite Central Committee program. David and Flo Harnish and children went to Tanzania under the umbrella of this program.

My brother Ralph is here too, his wife Carol, and their two children, Randy, 2, and Lisa, 6 months. He is not in TAP anymore but in a Columbia Teaching Program, but they've continued to invite them to TAP retreats.

Teacher's Abroad Retreat. Harnish family in lower left front.

Tonight we are having a "musical" evening, and we as a family are singing a Swahili song. The children know it very well, and I have bribed them with a promise of a present if they perform!! When we practiced, David sang right out, but time will tell. Actually we know quite a few Swahili songs by now—especially the melodies which the children have picked up. They can practically sing the entire liturgy but do not know the words. Some of the words are in Kibena, the tribal language. Once Dave tape-recorded a session in church, including the opening liturgy,

Ralph, Carol, Lisa Rheinheimer, son Randy standing in front. Kenya.

and there is David's little voice in one spot humming loudly!

We have had a very eventful trip since we left home; visited Serengeti; **many** wild animals with lions roaring just outside our tent; had enough mud to last our lifetime (David and Marie would not agree to that); slept one night out in the "bush" in a little house (unplanned but necessary); one night in the delivery rooms of a Catholic Hospital here in Kenya, because after we waited for a river to go down so we could pass, it was the nearest place with lights; a few days at Shirati; a few days in Nairobi; all very interesting in retrospect, but next time I wish we could **fly**. Esther Clemens is here.

On safari on the Serengeti. Lions sleeping in the plains. The Landrover did not disturb them.

I wonder what you are busily doing this season. We will miss you on the 24th of November. We got your Christmas box and are eagerly looking forward to opening it when we get back! We also received a package of magazines the **morning** we left, which I have absolutely devoured already.

Ralph, Randy and Carol Rheinheimer at Rheinheimer house in Kenya. Christmas, 1968.

Thank you, thank you, thank you!! I am working on the pillow kit you sent last year and love it! Many people here want to know where I got it.

Wish you were here! Blessed Christmas!!!! Don Jacobs' say "Hi!" Dave is writing business to Hiram. You will no doubt agree that I really **do** need a typewriter for my letters.

Love,
The Harnishes

JOURNALING:MUSINGS

Ilembula, 1968

I'm really not too sure when the whole idea of us coming here under MCC first began. Somehow since college days, it was always sort of in the back of my mind that "sometime" I should serve in some place. Well, then, Dave became too old to be drafted any more, since he had taken all those years of college, medical school, internship, and residency, but that somehow didn't seem right either. Then, when he finally finished the last years of the residency, we applied to MCC. Actually, I think maybe they applied to us. Periodically, we heard from them, at any rate. So we applied, and in due course of time, it was more or less settled where we would go, and when the departure date would be. It seemed like many things actually interfered with the departure date. Dave preferred going to an English speaking country, so he wouldn't need to learn another language. Actually, I would probably have chosen to learn the language [of the country], and enjoyed having the dividend of spending some time in Europe learning it. Since Aunt Mary Harnish had been in Tanzania for years, Dave sort of leaned towards coming here too. So in the end, it was decided to secund us to the Lutherans, who always seemed to be needing doctors, since Shirati at the moment seemed to be fairly well staffed with doctors.

After that we were eager to learn everything we could about Tanzania. Dorcas Stoltzfus happened to be on furlough in Philadelphia, so one night we invited her over for supper (to 111 Elfreth's Alley, Philadelphia). We had known her from her medical school days in Philadelphia. Well, she walked in the door and we immediately began plying her with questions. I can still remember us sitting, one on each side of her, on our living room davenport, talking and talking, when suddenly I realized we hadn't even had our supper yet! So then, we ate and talked, and talked some more. Mostly Dorcas talked about her work at Shirati, and we listened. But she made it seem so vivid, that for the first time, for me at any rate, it seemed like we had just paid a visit to Tanzania. It also made me truly realize that we had signed up for sure!

After that visit with Dorcas, things began to become very real. As we began to truly put our affairs in order, we began to get a little scared about this thing we had signed up to do. Tanzania seemed terribly far away from all the people we knew, and I began to really like our house there in Elfreth's Alley. And to think, we would be dragging our poor children away from all of their friends and from all that was familiar to them in this world! I began to feel like a real failure as a mother—that I would do such a thing to the children. Dorcas talked about snakes and all those things I dreaded so much, and I really think that during one period there, if we could have gotten out of our assignment without losing "face" we would have done so. After a while, I began to really face up to this change, and make some forward (instead of downward) progress, and in time began to look forward to coming; albeit, I think never without some qualms. I'm not really sure they've left me yet, to tell the truth. I often still feel quite strange here, and not at home, but I think I've felt that way ever since I left home at 18 to go to college. Where is my home anyway?

The funny thing is, now I have some of those same feelings about going back to the States next year! Here, the

Right: Just before departure to Tanzania. Florence, David, Anne, Marie, David Harnish. 1967.

Left: L to R: Marie Marguerite Harnish, Florence Rheinheimer Harnish, David Rollin Harnish. Passport pictures. Summer 1966.

children have had constant playmates—something they never had at home. It's true, they don't see their cousins but they don't really miss that—we miss it for them. Now and then I start talking to them about home, and get a sort of nostalgia, but they are often as puzzled as anything, and can't remember what I am talking about. Especially David.

Anyway, I sure remember that day of departure. We were to take an evening plane—Pan Am I think—from Philadelphia to London. Dave's parents and some of the family came to help us with last minute things. While it's true, there were many last minute things, still I had spent several months of frantic packing and planning, plus caring for the children. If it hadn't been for my good neighbors, Tom and Anne Kirchner, I really wonder how I would have managed. They helped me take care of the children many days so I could do other things. But, anyway, the day of departure arrived. We were finally packed up, and on our way to the airport with Paul, Dave's brother. Boy, were we surprised at all the people there, to see us off. Dave's entire family, except Ruth and Jerry, our friends the Hiram Hersheys, the Schrocks and others from Diamond Street Mennonite Church, Bill and Carolyn Mast, and others. There was a real crowd. They may have thought it was Mennonite Day at the Airport!

We had a little wait, but finally our plane was ready to load. They took our suitcases I think, and we kissed a few people (we're not really the kissing kind; Dave even kissed Tom Kirchner, which surprised me greatly), and then we walked to the plane—me clutching a very heavy "diaper bag" (there were books in the bottom because our suitcases were too heavy—a terrible mistake I discovered after lugging it around London and Rome!), and my poor lost stroller.

Even now, I could cry for that person who lost that stroller—me. For months before our departure, I had worried how we were going to transport an 8-month old baby, a 3-year old child, and a 5-year old child to all the places Dave wanted to see on our way over. Finally, I conceded to try a little travel, **IF** I could get a stroller. Dave wasn't in favor of it, and, since they cost quite a bit, I had to get it the best way I could, and that happened to be by Green Stamps. So Libby (my friend and neighbor on Elfreth's Alley) and I pored over Green Stamp books, and traded yellow for green, and compared values of strollers. Finally, I decided on one and dragged it halfway across town with the children, by bus, and even then, Dave wanted me to take it back. Well, I didn't take it back! I called a lot of airlines to see if they permitted strollers—I was always seeing these pictures of mothers wheeling their babies to the plane in a nice collapsible stroller. Most airlines said if it could be put under the seat it could be taken, but most also discouraged it. Well, I hung onto that stroller for dear life, although I was carrying Anne. I hadn't tagged it (a mistake) because I wasn't sure it could go on.

As we were walking to the plane, an airlines official said, "Here, I'll take care of that." I wanted to put a tag on then and there, but he said it wasn't necessary. Well, we got off at London, I saw them put the stroller on the cart with the other luggage, and that is the last I have ever seen of it! I just couldn't accept that, and we kept calling and calling from the place we stayed later, but it was never found. I must say, however, that later when we claimed the money for it from the airlines, they sent us the full amount; however, by that time, several months after we were here, our greatest need for it was over.

When we got on that first plane, I must admit there was a sort of queasy feeling in the pit of my stomach, due no doubt to all those headlines about all of those planes crashing and all those people being killed that were on board all those planes. Anyway, we anticipated receiving supper immediately, since we hadn't eaten since noon (live and learn, from now on I carry food with me—especially after being here in Tanzania a while), but it was around 11:00 P.M. until we finally got it. Poor children!

Then, I tried to bed them down beneath the seats, and I suppose they did as good as might be expected. Anne fared very well—she had the cutest little basket to sleep in, and even when we walked and carried her, she just slept when she was sleepy. I learned another thing about eating on airplanes—don't sit in the front on Pan Am because they start serving from the back, and don't sit in the back on Alitalia because they start serving from the front. Guess where we sat!

We were to arrive in London at 7:00 A.M. and we did. But what we didn't know beforehand was that it was 2:00 A.M. American time. We had heard various things said about losing time, etc., etc., and now I know why everybody always talked about it. We saw beautiful clouds and a beautiful sunrise through bleary eyes and were served beautiful orange juice and breakfast about two hours after eating a beautiful supper. We did not wake the children for that beautiful breakfast.

When we got off the plane—you have no idea how we were loaded down with luggage, for a six month stay—with everything, until the barrels arrived. We even had bought Marie and David air flight bags to put a few of their toys and books in which they were supposed to carry themselves. Marie did manage to lug hers around most of the time (I pitied her, really), but David just couldn't manage it. So Dave had David's air flight bag, his own suitcase camera case, and another duffel bag (something like that), and often David himself besides (after all, he was only three). I had Anne and my heavy bag, and Marie had her bag. We all were wearing coats, boots, hats, and everything we could **wear** besides. There were some very kind people traveling who helped us out, although I must say, Dave was very reluctant to let anyone touch any of our bags, although for myself, I welcomed it! However, I recall many minutes in which I and three children sat guarding our luggage while Dave went to make a phone call, or to get a taxi, or who knows what! I recall one tall, dignified Australian who was traveling to South Africa, who must have taken in this migration we were making, and saying to David, "Sonny, you'll really need those boots up there—it gets awfully foggy." This, as we were waiting to get on the plane in Rome to go to Nairobi. It was terribly hot there, and I suppose the remark illustrates well enough what an appearance we made!

As I was saying, when we got off the plane at London, David was so tired and sleepy, he just lost control of himself. We just had too much luggage, too little sleep, and too many children to cope with everything. All the way in to the customs place, and even after we got to the line of people waiting for customs (we were so slow we always wound up on the end of all lines), he SCREAMED, "I want a drink, I want a drink, I want a drink!" It was impossible to give him one there, although as I recall, I had just given him one, and finally someone who looked rather important took us and hustled us through customs ahead of all those other people. How grateful I was.

Finally I got him a drink, he took one **tiny** sip, but he did calm down a bit.

Somehow, in this family, a drink of water is symbolic of something. For whatever reason one is frustrated (from the viewpoint of the children), if they can just manage to holler for a drink, and get the parent to get it and to give it to them, it soothes. It is not the same if the child gets it himself, and, in fact, he usually refuses to do so. It must be handed to him—usually in the middle of the night, or in the middle of church.

After waiting around a while, Dave managed to find the place where MTS had arranged for us to stay. We waited and waited for the ill-fated stroller, which I so badly needed, but at last left. All the way to London proper from the airport, in the bus, we sang *London Bridge Is Falling Down*. We got to this place we were to stay, and it was on the top (fourth) floor—no elevators! We got all of us and all of our luggage up those stairs, but I don't know how many trips. They weren't just four flights either, but many curves and landings and flights. I counted them then, but now I have forgotten, thankfully.

Then, at last, we collapsed into bed and all slept soundly for three or four hours. Of course, no bed for Anne (and no stroller), so she slept in bureau drawers in London and Rome and was none the worse for it. Then, Dave insisted we go sightseeing! What I remember about London is cold, gray buildings, tiredness, walking with a baby, and double-decker buses. We did see Buckingham Palace and St. James Park, and got some pictures. I would like to spend some time there some day.

The next day, we were off to Rome. That trip was less traumatic. Shorter for one thing, and it was daytime. We got off at the airport and went to a place in town that was pretty snazzy for us. The proprietor could speak English well and said, "dollars" especially clearly. So, to our surprise, did everyone else in town.

Rome was pretty nice, really–those fountains where you can get a drink along the street captivated me and the children, although Dave wondered if it was safe to drink. We did and we survived. I don't know to this day if Dave drank any, though.

I always thought Rome was full of Popes and Catholics and things like that, but I didn't see any to speak of. There are beautiful statues, carvings, fountains, marvelous churches, the Appian Way, the unbelievable catacombs, and the fascinating Coliseum. Dave wouldn't take a ride on one of those horse-drawn carts, to our disappointment, however.

We stayed there for three days, and had a system after the first day. Dave went on tours all day. I went in the afternoon; after feeding the baby, doing the laundry, etc. For the second and third day we rented a stroller, and then I enjoyed it even more. One afternoon we took a walk by ourselves and maybe that was the nicest of all. David and Marie both rode in the stroller, and Dave carried Anne. I must say, I did get a little tired of that continental breakfast–coffee, rolls with butter and jam. And when you ask for milk for the children, it always comes as **hot** milk. About that time too, I began to run out of disposable diapers, and made haste to get some more! Fortunately Anne was still partly breastfed, or I don't know where I would have gotten milk and food for her in all our travels.

Although we had breakfast in the hotel, we got the other meals some place else. Dave always wanted spaghetti, which I only mildly like, but which was freely available. I always wanted pizza. Finally we found a place where we could get pizza, at a very Americanish tourist place. Imagine no Italian pizza in Italy!

From Rome we flew to Nairobi. Hershey Leaman and Nevin Kraybill met us at the airport. We felt strange to be in Africa anyway, and then to be met by a man with a beard. Was he really a Mennonite? At least we were thankful to be met for a change. I can't remember too much about that first arrival there because everything was so strange, and because all the memories of the Guest House are blurred together with the period of time we spent there while in Language School.

We stayed in Nairobi only a day or so and then flew to Shirati. Another thing about meals on planes – don't expect much on East African Airways. Guess there's not too much space for food after you get all those baby chicks, people, and luggage aboard. Everything is in plain sight, and you can really keep track of your luggage. Nevin was driving back to Shirati, new car I think, and thought maybe Dave would drive out with him in the car (12-hour journey) and we'd come by plane as scheduled, but Dave demurred. You'll have to ask him why; I'm not sure. Anyway, Nevin was surprised (I think) and went on ahead. I thought it would be sort of fun to travel with the children alone, if it was only that one short hop, and there would be someone to put us on and meet us.

Our stay in Tanzania, East Africa was from 1967 to 1970. Dave served as surgeon and medical director of a 200-bed hospital. The hospital was located in the beautiful southern highlands of Tanzania where we had an ideal climate the year round. There we came in contact with the extraordinary people and their culture.

We had been conditioned by "missionary" stories of "primitive" people who live in mud houses. We were, therefore, very pleasantly surprised by some aspects of our life here. As we became acquainted with the people and their way of life, we gained an appreciation of their culture as being of equal importance to our own. We were encountering the effects of early missionaries and settlers, both good and bad, in their attempts to evangelize, but also acculturate another people. Today Africans and other people are beginning to realize that Christianity is not the same as westernization, and that everything African is not "heathen." There is a dawning realization of the African culture as beautiful, with roots going many centuries back. African culture is much older than American culture, if antiquity adds value.

Africans make many things of beauty, a few of which we will bring back. The pottery is lovely to look at as well as very functional. Pots of beautiful symmetry are created from lumps of clay, time after time, by illiterate women from clay that they dug from the earth themselves. One place located close to the hospital seemed to be a place where women gathered to make pottery. I haunted this spot because it was fascinating to watch the women at work. I tried making pots myself a time or two, but was completely embarrassed by my failure. The pots are made as water jugs and cooking utensils, and are a source of income. The poverty in this area can be illustrated by the fact that these vessels are sold for from 7 cents to 40 or 50 cents (in dollars). The women considered them as functional, as well as decorative, because there was usually a distinctive design of some type around the pots, made perhaps with a piece of stone, a sea shell, or a coin. It reminds me a little bit of Pennsylvania Dutch pies—the pie tastes the same without ornament, but most pie makers pride themselves on their own little decorative touches.

The basketry of the various tribes is a wonder to behold. An expert would be able to identify a basket by its design, and state which tribe it came from. The baskets are very functional in everyday life for carrying things on the head. Nevertheless each basket has its own design woven in, usually quite intricate. They are made from the grasses of various types. Some dyes, used for the designs, are made from roots of trees and shrubs, others are purchased. Lovely hanging baskets are made to suspend food and belongings to protect them from marauders—either insects or animals.

Wooden carvings are widely recognized as being part of African culture. Various types of wood are used for these. Perhaps the most famous carvers in East Africa are the Wakonde, who use black ebony for their carvings. Certain carved objects are functional, such as spoons and bowls, others such as carvings of people and animals, are artistic and made for the tourist market. The life of rural Africa is depicted by some of these carvings.

JOURNALING:SEWING CLASS

1968

Ilembula

❖ ❖ ❖ ❖ ❖

*M*y sewing class really began last year, when the woman medical doctor from Holland and I got started together. First, for several weeks, we tried to contact the *Mama Mkuu* (the president) of the mother's organization. Finally, she was located and came here for a talk with us. Our Swahili wasn't so hot just then, so the conversation was rather limited, although I think we got the point across, and she said, "thank you very much, we are grateful."

That first meeting, we had prayer and singing before we got started, but since then we just start right in without all that wasted time. Wasted time? Anyway, time is limited, and sometimes the singing is spontaneous. That's probably better anyway.

I must say, several months later, at the moment, I don't know if I am more upset or enthused about this sewing class of mine. Today Mama M---- came. The ostensible reason was to ask me for money for the *jmfuko wa wamama* (to pay to the office at Njombe.)

I had been asked before if I would contribute, and I said that I would; however, up to this point I hadn't contributed, therefore I was glad to do it. The day they all gave beans, somehow or other I missed it in church, which is just as well since I didn't have any beans to give. I must say, however, that one does wonder exactly what will become of this money, and how it will be spent. Not that **I** gave so much, only Sh. 5/- (less than a dollar).

So then we got to talking about the sewing class. She is the president of the association. She said that many of the women had taken two or more of the pieces of material along home with them. However, it had been decided (actually, I decided it because they forced me into it), that they could choose one piece, write their names on it, and leave it here in the box until I was able to help them cut and sew. I knew that at least one or two had taken theirs with them, among them Mama M---- **herself**, but I did not know to what extent. Now, I have no objection to some of these women who cannot afford to pay for this material if they get it free. But I **do** object to them stealing it by hiding it under their *kangas*; in my opinion this is not conduct becoming to the life of a Christian, but is in actuality deceit. Forgive me, but I have a strong suspicion the real reason for this objection to the others' taking cloth is that they were left behind, and didn't get any.

So, they want me to watch carefully so that no one can steal. This, of course, is exactly the kind of thing I would like to avoid. On all sides you hear the cry "*Uhuru*," and, "Down with the White Man," yet I have these women asking me if I will police them! I asked Mama M---- and Bahtletti, who was also present (necessarily, as I will explain later), if they wanted **me**, a stranger in their midst, working amongst Christians, to act as their policeman. I explained that I had come to help them to learn to sew, and if they took the cloth, then that was stealing on their part, and not a sin of mine (*Si kosa yangu*). They agreed, and Mama M---- said that **she** would do the policing. Once before she had agreed to write down the names, but nothing came of it. So we shall see. They want me to put out only a few at a time—*i.e.*, of the pieces of cloth, and say that you, and you, and you, may have this, or this, or this.

Perhaps I have been very naïve by placing so much material out at a time. Somehow, although it is true that I want the people who cannot afford to buy it, to have this material, still I seem to want to give it to them, rather than to have them just take it. The trouble is I suppose, that I am afraid those who get it are those who do not need it. But, *kumbe*, according to our standards they all need it. So what's the matter then? Why don't I just lay the cloth out and say, "Here, help yourself." Actually, if I thought they wouldn't be greedy, I would probably do this.

I don't like to talk about this problem to the other missionaries (here), because they have been telling me all along that the local people are thieves, liars, and want to trick you. Missionaries mostly who reason thus, if pressed with a specific example of someone who is **not** a thief, liar, and trickster, will usually concede that yes, there may be such a good person, but he is very rare. They then proceed to tell about all the instances in which they themselves have been stolen from, lied to, and tricked. Most of these instances, in my opinion, are usually their own fault and as a result of their trying to take advantage of the other person. Now what I am trying to say is this: it has been my contention that the people here are the same kind of people as all of us are; some of them are indeed thieves and liars, but others, and the majority I believe, are good, kind, helpful people, just like people anywhere. Therefore, if I then discuss this particular problem I am having, they will say, "Oh yes, didn't we tell you so?"

This Friday, I have invited the entire group here for tea. However, I am beginning to feel compelled to give a talk in Swahili—something about stealing. Perhaps the story of Matthew. Is this God's leading? I do so want to be a witness for Him here, both for the sake of God, as well as for the sake of all white people who have oppressed other peoples. And for black people as well who have oppressed other peoples.

Can I expect to make any sort of impact here? No. But I have to try.

At the moment, I am also thinking about trying to arrange some sort of "health" lectures; on preventable disease, healthful foods, perhaps family planning, building of privies, etc. I wish I could speak a little better Swahili, but probably that is only an excuse. I think I know enough now that I could go ahead with at least a lecture, although I would have difficulty with any kind of discussion, which I feel is very desirable. This leads me to explain why I said that Bahtletti was necessary when I speak to Mama M----. I have always had some trouble communicating with Mama M----. Today I asked Bahtletti if it was just me, or if she, Mama M----, didn't speak such good Swahili. I got my clue from the fact that Mama M---- asked me if I, **too**, thought Kiswahili was *kigumu* (difficult). I realized then that she was having some trouble with Kiswahili herself and it wasn't all me. Then when I asked Bahtletti about it, she said that she often laughs because Mama M---- mixes up Kibena with her Kiswahili and that is why I have difficulty in understanding. Bahtletti translates for me, and I have little difficulty understanding her. Also, she has become used to my particular speech idiosyncrasies, and corrects me, at my request.

Coming back to the sewing class. If I know these things, *i.e.,* that they have more or less "stolen" the cloth, don't treat members of other tribes too kindly (at least in one instance here), and do not in any sense of the word take turns, why do I continue? Incidentally, I might also mention that one of our newly purchased (with our own money) scissors is missing. Nevertheless, when I see someone come back with a nicely sewn garment, I am so pleased and just want to show everyone how well that person has done! It's trite to say that this is rewarding, but it is true. Those who have stolen, well, the sin is on their heads, not mine. And if there are a few who really learn to sew well, and in this way to help themselves and their families, I am nothing if not grateful.

So, therefore, I am able to say that on the whole, I am very enthused and willing to put a lot of time into this sewing project. Not, I hope, at the expense of the family however. There are a few who have really learned to sew well in my opinion, and for these few, it is well worth it. The others, well, many have gotten new garments, and although they may not be sewn really well, still on the whole, they are quite presentable. New clothes, plus learning to sew if even a little bit, is worthwhile.

From the money they have paid, we have about half enough now to buy the cheapest sewing machine available in Dar, according to Harold Miller. So, you see, we have great ambitions. You understand, of course, that all of the sewing up to this point has been done by hand. Bahtletti has a machine in her home, and she is the one exception to this. She has learned to sew fairly well too, although she had done some before. I might mention that she has also made a quilt top, patchwork style, which to my undiscerning eye looks quite beautiful and adequate. She had asked me to buy one of the MCC quilts from the hospital one day (we use MCC quilts on our beds here as well as in our guest rooms), but I told her I did not think they were for sale, and encouraged her to make one of her own. I even promised to get her the backing material if she made one. Well, I have been giving her various scraps of mine and others, and lo and behold, if she didn't make a very adequate quilt! So now I have to get her some backing material someplace. I don't know yet where that will come from. There is one thing about the quilt, you can't get it folded properly, and I finally concluded that it wasn't quite rectangular some place or other. Seems like I recall my Mom used to have that trouble a little sometimes too. Anyway, I am very proud of her, she has certainly done something I have never attempted. So now maybe I'll have to get her some more scraps. She is really quite fond and proud of it herself.

LETTERS

1969

January 6, 1969
Ilembula, Tanzania

Dear Hersheys,

Just a note in addition to Marie's "thank you" to let you
know how absolutely **delighted** we are with the gifts you
sent us. The girls have already spent hours with their dolls,
and Marie combs and combs hers. When she opened the
box she said, "Just what I wanted," absolutely spontaneously! The little train for David is just about the cutest
thing we have ever seen, and he loves it (so does Anne and
Marie—and Daddy). As to the sweater, you couldn't have
pleased me more! So thanks very, very much.

We are pretty healthy, although I have gotten my stupid
rash (allergy?) back and currently my face is hot, itchy, and
swollen. David said, "Your red eye is the baddest, Mommy!"
David has a cold too—not bad.

We had to stay with friends in Dodoma, as we just
couldn't get back here in time. We really had a good time
with them. I should tell you about our Santa Claus deal—

Of course, Dave rang the bells. He ran around the house, ringing them—then came into the house with a big bag of toys.

they rigged up bells, and then put gifts outside. David insists Santa came, but Marie wasn't so sure, but she "just wanted to know who rang those bells." No more space now.

Love,
Flo Harnish

February 1, 1969
Ilembula, Tanzania

Dear Janie,

The church women asked me if I would read or say some words at their Wednesday morning meeting. I read (Swahili), and was most pleased to be asked. I hope to resume sewing soon—the women are focusing now on the rains.

I forgot to mention the last time that I had finally received that packet of books (mostly about children) and I read them all already, except parts of *Your Inner Child of the Past*. When I say finally, it is because I had been looking forward to them—they did seem to take longer than usual to get here. I agree with you in that I like Holt, although I think he's a little long on principle and a little short on specific fact. I'm not too sure why I'm reading all these books on child care, but my rationale is that while I'm in Nursing School I read nursing books, while I am rearing children I read books on rearing children. But the thing that bothers me is why do some of these people never have to read any of these books, and yet do such a better job of child-rearing than I do?!

Also, I have received a packet of magazines from you which I am not sure I thanked you for (and I DO thank you—it gives me a real boost and contact with home to get these magazines), and the last most delightful thing we have received from you are those *Little Bear* books. They are really nice! The children love them, and I must confess I read them through quickly too to see what they're about. Marie can read some of them and with a little help about all of them. I don't know why, but she seems reluctant to try sometimes when I'm almost sure she can do certain things. Why is this? Am I pushing her? Anyway, we do thank you for all these books, magazines, toys, and other things you have sent. I wish there were a better way of expressing it than with words!

MCC clothes distribution have caused real headaches!

Speaking of reading nursing books in Nursing School—how are you coming, you poor thing! What a schedule you must have! I'll never forget that hectic year at Penn, and I didn't have **any** children most of the time. Are you taking a heavy load again this semester? (I know that dates me terribly, nowadays they say trimester, right?)

It was decided, by the Mistress of Nursing and Dave: Bwana Mkubwa (Mr. Big) to distribute some clothing, lovingly sent by MCC–US. The things were getting moldy for one thing, in the storehouse. The layette bundles were given as incentives to women to entice them to give birth in the hospital, but, in my mind, the most needy, who couldn't afford to come to the hospital, didn't receive them. How I wanted to go to the villages to give them to the most needy, but that opportunity didn't present itself to me for various reasons. And the bundles weren't always used the way intended. I saw several blankets used as head wraps. Once, I bought eggs at the door (eggs found some place, probably) tied in a neat layette blanket package. Also saw some layette blankets used as headgear by women.

I forgot to mention also, that the pictures of Peter and Tommy taken in school are really good! Did you have a Christmas picture besides that one? Of all years we should have sent one, this year we didn't!

I'll bet you will really miss Glen and JoAnn. Hope we get to see them sometime when they get to Pennsylvania again—tell JoAnn I tried her Martha Washington bread one time, but it wasn't nearly as good as when she made it! If you see them yet, before they go, that is.

Harold and Esther Kraybill have adopted a Korean child. They are in Korea now. (He's a doctor, younger than we are, and we had met them in Philadelphia.) They will be home this summer, I believe. Also, one of Dave's cousins, Arlene and John Weber, a builder in Lancaster County, have also adopted a Korean child, about 6 months old I think, just before Christmas.

Yesterday morning when Charles (our Tanzanian boy-helper) went to feed the rabbits, there was an 8 to 9 ft. python sleeping in one of the cages! It had eaten a large white rabbit (borrowed!) and after they (pythons) eat they are very sluggish. Also, after they eat, they cannot get out of the same small holes they get into, since they swallow whole. We are not quite as afraid of the pythons as we are of some of the other snakes, because their bite is not actually poisonous—they squeeze. Dave and one of the Tanzania medical staff killed it. Dave pinned it down with something (after lifting it out of the cage in a large tin kerosene can) and the other man cut off its head with a shovel. This however, spited Dave, because he is skinning it now and wanted the head on! I will have nothing to do with this skinning, but Dave has "captivated" David and Marie to help. David complained to me later that even though he washed his hands with soap, he still smelled like snake!

We have heard of some missionaries who have eaten python steaks. I am having a hard time convincing Anne of their danger, when she sees them handling them like that, but maybe she comprehends. She just came in and said, "He's dead. He don't move!" Last week either a spitting cobra or a

Waiting for plane carrying "Flying Doctors," after clearing airstrip of rocks, cattle, etc. Dr. Harnish, white coat and bare feet, carried Marie Harnish, right foreground, through small stream in Ilembula.

black mamba killed one of our neighbor's sitting ducks to get at the duck eggs. The black mambas are really lethal, if it was that. However, as we have been assured many times, snakes don't attack unless provoked! Statistically speaking, they are far less to be feared than car accidents in the States. Mrs. L_____, the mother of six from age 9 to 6 months, expresses absolutely no fear of them for her children. She says we live in a very safe environment here. Perhaps we do.

The flying doctors were here Friday until this morning. This is always a great day for the children. Dave usually lets them go along to inspect the airstrip for cows and stones and to fetch and to return the doctors to the plane. This time there was an older surgeon from Oregon along, and a nurse from Switzerland. The pilot is the same one who has been here now quite a few times. I have come to one conclusion: all pilots should be called Pilot Jim, because they all seem to be named Jim.

I have been meaning to say, if that "thing" I sent you is broken or cracked when it arrives do not worry. It is not expensive, in fact very cheap. They do crack easily and I sent this more or less as a test case. I hope the things soon arrive, especially since they were sent as Christmas presents.

Please tell us something you would especially like from here! Mrs. F. did get the book and thank you so much. Unfortunately she had already stopped nursing and I hope she will give the book to me. There have been many times when I wished I would have it. The children and I continue to enjoy our Christmas gifts.

Love, Flo

February 24, 1969
Ilembula, Tanzania

Dear Janie,

How delighted I was to get your letter. It seems like we don't hear from you nearly often enough. By this I don't mean papers, books, etc., but actual letters. But, with your previous schedule, I don't see how you even ground out any letters at all. I sometimes wish you were here (of course just to talk things over because I miss that and need your opinion), but simply because there is so much to be done, and you have so much energy and efficiency. Please take that as a compliment! I feel guilty about many things. (1) I don't know the language as well as I should by this time (probably as good as the average), (2) Even with the language I do know, I could do so much more, (3) I am a teacher in nursing schools, and this nursing school needs teachers (I could teach as much as I wanted to, and am just now toying with the idea of teaching one course), (4) The people should be taught to sew, sew, sew, (5) The people should be taught the simple elements of hygiene and nutritious cooking, (6) I should attend the early morning prayer services, (7) I should spend more creative time with the children, (8) I should spend more time in private Bible study, (9) etc., etc.

About teaching them to sew—we have suspended operations for the moment (with the exception of one lady) because we had run out of material, then we went on safari in December, now it is the rainy season, and these women can't leave their *shambas* (their fields, or gardens) because they are principally responsible for the farming, although I believe some of the men do help these days. Don't let anyone tell you that the women lead an easy life. They are in their *shambas* from early morning until night. Sometimes they have a child strapped to the back, and sometimes they have one inside, and I suspect sometimes they have both. Some women are one of several wives, so you can see how much help they can expect from a husband like that. For them to farm is a simple matter of survival.

Second from left, Flo in outskirts of village of Ilembula.

In this area, there is no true starvation or famine such as in India for example. Anyone who is willing to work (hard) can get food. There are cases of *Kwashiorkor* (protein deficiency) here, but possibly due to lack of nutritional knowledge, and perhaps due to lack of cash in hand to buy meat. One of the things that has broken my heart here has been the people asking for work of any kind. It is not laziness that has made trouble for them, but something else I can't put my finger on. Dave and I have discussed (argued, is probably more accurate) as to who has worked the hardest—these people here who carry water for miles on their heads, do most of their farming with a *jembe* (like a big hoe) although a few do use oxen or cows (I've never quite understood the difference between cows and oxen), then they harvest their rice, corn, roots, beans, and grind them by hand in big mortars and pestles—usually two women working together (I think, never the men). By the way, Dave thinks that would be a good reducing exercise for me.

Later, I realized there is indeed starvation.

It is true, however, that they have very little housework, such as you and I spend a great deal of our energy on. Oh, I forgot to mention that they cook **all** of their food, except fruit, and that means they must have loads and loads of wood carried from afar to make all of these fires. This too is the work of the women for the most part, as far as I have been able to observe (must admit, that's probably not too far). But Dave claims that Lancaster County

Women grinding grain into fine powder. The poles are very heavy.

farmers work harder, especially during harvest season—I claim they don't. And so it goes, round and round. We have been driving along the road in the early morning and see people carrying huge loads on their heads, on their way to market. This is before day, mind you. I had heard that part of the economic problem here is that the people are lazy, but I have changed my mind. One must also remember that many of these people have chronic illnesses, and probably don't feel good much of the time.

And about teaching them hygiene. How would you tell a mother to wash her hands with soap every time after changing the baby, for example, if she has to carry all her water from the river, and then to boil it, if she boils it. This past weekend Marie had a rather severe diarrhea (by today she is fine again), but all I could think of as I carried her to the bathroom all last Thursday night (she had a temp of 103 degrees and was too weak and dizzy to stand) was how do the Africans cope with this kind of illness, which they have so much. And it is always more prevalent in the dry season, when they can't catch the water from the rains near their homes. It seems to me that the first thing to do when you are trying to teach hygiene here, is to dig wells for everybody! Of course I'm very ignorant of these engineering matters, and I'm sure there must be a perfectly valid reason why this has not been done, and why it can't be done today.

About teaching nutrition, for them, meat is terribly, terribly expensive, although for us it costs about 17 cents a pound in American money; in their money it would be Shs. 1.20 per pound, which I suppose in buying power for them compares roughly to 1.20 a pound in dollars and cents (this typewriter does not have a dollar sign, only the English £ symbol). So, I don't know just how much meat the poorer people eat. Also, I have been surprised that they eat many green vegetables, as well as peanuts, peanut leaves, some sweet potatoes, and tomatoes, which grow wild around here. They also eat many fruits, but only a few deliberately plant fruit trees, or so it seems to us. Here at the mission there are many fruit trees, but the others seem to be only as the winds must have buffeted the seed about—with of course several big exceptions. We find many small lemon or orange or other fruit trees here, and we usually try to give them to someone, but don't know what their further fate is. I wonder if the U.S. Government Printing Office, or Foreign Service Office, or some such branch of official Washington might have some statistics about nutritional content of the fruits here: mangoes (I think I'm allergic to them and I love them!), guavas, papaya, etc. Would you have any idea about that? The Heinz booklet, *Nutritional Values,* might have it, but unfortunately I don't have my copy here. Seasonally, at least, I think the people here really do get plenty of vitamins. They eat lemons and oranges, skin and all, so do Dave, Marie, David, Anne, but not me. Too bitter.

I was pleased that about two weeks ago, the president of the women's organization there asked me when I would be ready to help them out in their morning prayers. I told her I was ready to read—actually Swahili is very phonetic—if you hear it, you can write it. So I did read II Corinthians 13, but I chickened out on saying any words. Nevertheless, I did feel accepted, and the leader seemed real pleased. Sometimes we get the feeling around here that we are more tolerated than loved (especially from the younger aspiring element) but these church ladies did not give me that feeling—actually there were only a handful there.

This is now February 29th.

I sure do write some mixed up letters. Last Sunday, to continue my wanderings, we went to a different church. It was a "country" church with thatched roof, mud walls, the usual mud benches (but hard as cement) with no backs, and cave-like entrance with small windows, dark interior until your eyes got used to it. We were ushered right up to the front, under protest. The children did fairly well, and Anne only fell off of her three-legged stool three times, until I made her sit on a bench with me. They had a normal sermon, baptism (the three infants squalled during the whole service), and communion. It was long, and after the sermon and baptism, the children and I did not go back in, but sat in Harry L___'s bus (we went with him—he is pastor as well as builder—more before the nationalization than now). They had communion with a common cup, but fortunately Dave sat near the front, and was one of the first. We are really squeamish about some things, and must get over it! Guess we know and see a little too much in the hospital.

The children and I were surrounded by children in the car, who were watching our every move. This is the usual thing. Marie and David don't like that too well, but Anne just loves it, and really shows off. Here is what I wrote at the time, having started a letter to you: "We are sitting in Harry L___'s car with a group of African children surrounding us, and watching our every move. They laugh very much when Anne who is eating an apple, spits seeds or peelings out the window. There is one boy who is walking with a stick—sort of hopping with the other foot. You see many children like this, some even sort of walking on their hands in a squatting position with their legs dangling along. They go very fast, whatever position they maneuver in. This particular boy seems very friendly and has an intelligent attractive face, smiling much, but watching our every move. He looks about the size of a 7- or 8-year-old child, but when I asked him his age, he said he was 12. He said he's in the first grade this year, and able to read now. It's not an unusual age to begin school. To go to school here there are many factors; you have to pay for one thing, so if the parents don't have the money or are disinclined to send the child, he is just out of luck. So differ-ent from the States where parents are arrested for **not** sending children to school."

"The people have come out of the church now, including Harry, and they are walking someplace, single file, through the cornfields towards a place where I think they will eat *ugali*. (The staple of the diet here—like very thickened flour.)

In the meantime (I'm just remembering now, because I got out of the car then to watch what I am going to describe) the young people, mostly girls, oh maybe 15 to 20, began to sing and dance outside the church. They formed a circle, not touching each other, and first they danced around this way with certain steps, then turned around and went the other way. They were singing, and as is frequent with their singing they had a leader and then the others joined in. It was close to what we would probably describe as folk dancing, but there were no couples. It was very lovely to see. We never have anything of that type outside our great big German-built church here.

Ugali is made from manioc.

However, something that amazed us very much, was one of the songs they were singing—in English: "I love, I love you baby. Do you love me baby? Do you kiss me baby?!!" I am quite sure they did not really realize what they were singing, except perhaps the gist of it. I don't know. A couple of them rode home part way with us and Harry, and I tried to ask them if they knew what those words meant, but Dave made me stop asking! Just like a husband! One boy did say that they can say words but they don't know what they mean. A little like us when we sing out of the Swahili or Kibena hymnal at church! Anyway, they sang a long time, and then someone came and invited us to tea, but I was really sorry because I would have watched them for a long time. But, drinking tea always with much milk and sugar, we got cups with saucers. I noticed after Harry finished his cup, the cup was filled immediately, without washing, and given to an old blind man. We were really honored to be asked, it happens rarely.

The official language in their schools at that time was English

Watch your post for next installment.
Flo

March 3, 1969
Ilembula, Tanzania

Now just must finish this today.

Dave wants me to ask you if you are able to get frames for 35mm slides, similar to Kodak. Either plastic or cardboard.

Do you know of any organization off-hand that would consider financing a foreign student for undergraduate school and medical school? One of the medical assistants here has been accepted at Augustana College in Wisconsin (I think, or farther west) but has no money, and the church has refused here to loan or support him (frankly, they don't have that kind of money either).

Have you seen the Kirchners lately? We haven't heard from them for a while except a note the middle of January, saying they were sick.

That other package from you came in the last post—Thursday. The children are mad about those colored pens. Marie can absolutely not let them alone, and is mass producing pictures around here. She has promised that I may send one to you, but I can't include it in this air form. Thank you very much. Also, they seemed willing to put their presents away until their birthdays, but **I** peeked! They are great. You certainly shouldn't have sent anything, but they will really like those things! I will tell you their reactions later!

Two books which I have read lately (my sister sent them, Rae) and that I would recommend to you are *Christy* by Catherine Marshall, and *God's Smuggler* by Brother Andrew. They are both pocket editions, and I thought them very good.

Rangnar (Swedish) and Marie Harnish playing with colored pencils sent by Mary Jane Lederach Hershey.

The handshake here is like this: first shake hands normally, then shake each other's thumbs, then shake hands normally again! Try it, it gives a rather strange sensation. At first, I didn't know what to think! They also have some kind of finger snapping ritual which I haven't mastered, and don't intend to try.

How are the gerbils doing? I did read about them in the Creative Playthings catalogue before we left. They sound very nice. Our children continue their interest, along with their father, in gardening and animal raising. Our German neighbor has baby ducks, baby rabbits, baby chickens, baby turkeys, and everything in her garden grows just great. She claims it's because she is a midwife. Also, Dave has been having a series of several Caesarian Sections again, and he claims that is because it is a full moon. You see, we are quite superstitious here.

Right now our children have gone over to the L_____'s laundry room to swim and bathe. They (and we too) wash on Mondays, so that means the boiler is nice and hot with warm water from the fire in the morning. I have never seen them playing in there, but Mrs. L. says they plug up the drain with something, put water all over the floor, and then scoot around on their bare hinies and have a great time. She said one time Rangnar, 6, had a really sore bottom from this activity, but our three have not complained of that particular ailment.

Marie is dying for a two-wheeler, because Rangnar has one. She is trying to learn on his. It's actually a little sandy and hilly here, but many people do have them. We do have a large English type tricycle with hand brakes and springs and things, and it is as large as a small two wheeler. Dave just (re) fixed it on Saturday again, so we've been hearing a lot of squalling about people who won't take turns. This of course includes other children besides our own.

The Fisher family is spending a few weeks here from Njombe. She is the woman you had sent the booklet on breast-feeding too. She has returned the book now, and she said she would

David Harnish riding tricycle at Ilembula.

write to you—she said you sent her a very nice letter. I'm not too sure how much it has helped her—she seemed a little puzzled in some ways, but said she got some good ideas from it.

I am discovering that the German philosophy of rearing children differs a good bit from ours. She thought that picture was very amusing that showed the baby in a slanting seat in the midst of much family activity. I think yesterday was a typical schedule for her 6-month old. She went to church in the morning (baby at home) then all the missionaries here were invited to the L____'s for dinner (baby at home), then she came back after having gone to feed the baby (baby at home). Left alone a good bit of the time.

I think that I will try to send the book now to Annetta Miller in Dar es Salaam. She (Mrs. Harold, with Eastern Board) has given birth to their first children, twins, boy and girl, **each** weighed 7 lbs. 13 oz.! They were just home on furlough, and I'm sure she didn't get back much more than a month before their birth. You thought **you** had a big baby. (And I thought **I** did.)

We're in good, I should say, excellent health at the moment. We may be in a mid-term slump, or else we're beginning to find out a little too much about the problems here! Do write. I didn't edit this—it has to go.

Love, Flo

April 19, 1969
Ilembula, Tanzania

Dear Janie,

How pleased again to get your informative letter. We had about given up on getting any mail from America for the past several weeks! For the last several months we have been feeling the effects of the dock strike (we presume) and haven't gotten a single magazine or package of any type that wasn't airmailed. Nobody much wrote to us lately, and even our parents failed us for a few weeks. Today we got letters from both parents, you, a friend in Sweden (from here), MCC and so we feel a little bit more "remembered."

We're fine, except for some sniffling noses and stomach cramps. Nothing to put us into bed! It's Saturday afternoon and David and Marie are out playing someplace and Anne is still sleeping. It sure is nice still to have one child to take naps with! That Anne, she's something. The other day she was saying something like "Oont, Esther." When I asked her what that meant she said, "That's Swedish!" It is, too. Marie knows what it means but won't tell me. I found out its much like "ouch!" Nothing pleases David and Marie more than to say something in Swedish that Dave and I can't understand! A switch from where the parents know a language and the children don't. We can't say anything in Swahili anymore to each other that we don't want them to know. And coming back to Anne, today she and Esther were hanging on to Bahtletti's skirt (our housegirl) and all three were laughing, and they were saying something that sounded like "Eh heh" Bahtletti laughed and said to me that they were saying the Kibena (tribal language here) word for "get away from me!"

I'm glad you finally got our "Christmas package." Too bad that pot was broken. It's really discouraging, because I am very fond of them, and am always buying them. Now I just don't know how I will get them home. I use them in the house for water, onions, tomatoes, bread, casseroles, etc., etc.

My sewing class has renewed now, and I feel very hopeful about it. We meet every Friday from about 3:00 P.M. until dusk, which is around 7:00 P.M. Yesterday they all made brassieres—all the same size (!), and were very pleased with themselves. They are not yet finished, and I will be most anxious to see how useful they really will be. They seem awfully small to me, but I guess I have my own reasons for thinking that. But my class is just like anywhere else—some really listen and pay attention, and know what they are doing. Others wander about when you are talking and then say they can't do it! Now, as to needs of this sewing class—yes, I am in much need of materials. There is a problem however, considering how long it takes for packages to get here, if you plan to send it, it should be sent now, hoping it doesn't get tied up someplace. Otherwise it won't be of use to me, although there would be others who could use it I am positive. Other needs are elastic, and scissors. I don't know of anyone except Bahtletti, who owns her own scissors.

I am very grateful to you for your pattern and at least six or so have made shifts, and Bahtletti has made a shirtwaist. Many have made panties for children, and shirts and shorts, and these simple straight dresses for girls—they tend to want more fancy ones, but I encourage them to sew the simple ones. I try to give all of them the pattern from newspapers. I enjoy the class, and feel a little like you do about your Jefferson class—it may be one of the most meaningful things I have done.

Any material that you might send should be river-washable! Little ironing is done, although you'd be surprised how nice they manage to make their clothes look with their charcoal irons. Have you ever seen a charcoal iron? Once, shortly before we came, I got some material on Second Street between Elfreth's Alley and Market Street on the west side for something like 50 cents or 65 cents a yard—it was absolutely drip-dry of some type, and it was really great! We are still using it. Something like that would be wonderful. Another possibility would be if I would buy the material myself here in Njombe, Mbeya or someplace. You can get material here, although it is not as nice, and more expensive. However, considering shipping charges, I guess it wouldn't be. If you do send something, be sure to send it like this:

	For use by:
Harold Miller	Mrs. David Harnish
Christian Council of Tanzania	Ilembula Lutheran Hospital
P.O. Box 2537, Dar es Salaam	P.B. Iringa, Tanzania
East Africa	

Otherwise, we will have to pay customs.

As for us, we are thinking in terms of packing to come home, so I do not encourage anyone to send more things for us, unless it be something that we will pass on and leave here. If there is something really urgent we need, I will let you know, but generally speaking, we are quite comfortable. Marie loved her birthday sewing kit, and we sat down and sorted it all out, and she promptly did the "A." I wish I could do it for her, it's so much fun, but she won't let me touch it. Yesterday was David's birthday, and was he pleased with those boats! He spent the afternoon playing in the tub, and today they had a big mud hole out front with the other children and were playing. They sure do make some cute toys these days. Thank you very much! By the way, I am almost done with that sweater! Isn't that unbelievable? I put my embroidery aside (although I shall soon resume it now) and just worked on the sweater. I have the bottom ribbing to finish, the neck ribbing, and the buttons.

Come, come, come. You wouldn't really let Hiram come without you, would you!!!

Love, Flo

Party time. David Harnish, facing, second child from left; Anne Harnish, 2nd child from right; Marie Harnish, center front with back to camera. Right, and center back, Swedish children. Two children to left, local boys.

May 19, 1969
Ilembula, Tanzania

Dear Elaine (Unzicker),

It was good to hear from you. It's really exciting to us to think you might come here! Answering your questions. We thought two barrels inadequate for our three children, so took another one, but if I'm correct, we had to pay for it ourselves. I'll ask Dave. Weather: temperature here is about ideal in our opinion! It ranges from about 60 to 90 degrees, as Dave mentioned. On cool morning and evenings, sweaters, hooded jackets, and something on the legs of the children are good.

If you go to Language School in Nairobi, and if TAP retreat continues to be held at Limuru, you really need quite warm clothing for the children. Our children were kept outside on the lawn all day at Language School, and I wrote home to my mother to send hooded jackets for the children, and tights for the girls. At that time they had no indoor facilities for the children, although I hear that now they do have some sort of shelter built. I had some misgivings about how much I would get out of language school with three children (at that time their ages were 5, 3, and 8 months), but it worked out fine. They put beds out for those that are still needing naps, and at noon we usually took our lunch from the Mennonite Guest House and ate together there under the trees in a leisurely fashion. Some of the others went home to eat, but that was a mad scramble—traffic-wise, although they got better food. We considered language school a great privilege, and were the only TAPPERS who got to go for three months. And here, in the "bush," it is quite necessary.

The nights are always cool, and even cold—never really hot at night here—typical mountains, so you do need warm pajamas at some times of the year. It is just going into the cool season now, and I have put one blanket on our bed, and the children are in their warm pajamas. We also have quilts on the beds. Boots and raincoats are very useful. We put the same kind of shoes on the children as at home, mostly sneakers! Sandals are also good. We hardly ever put really heavy shoes on them, although at some of the other mission stations, the children do wear heavy shoes. Now, when we first came, we were so careful that they had shoes on at every minute, but now we find that they wear these little "flip-flops" (as we call them—they're these little rubber thongs) all the time, or even go barefoot if they can get by with it. It's probably not too good of an idea to let them go barefoot, but they do, if they can get by with it. The Swedish missionary children hardly ever have a shoe on their feet! You can get thongs, sandals, and sneakers here in the towns. The only trouble we have had is once when Anne, our youngest, got some kind of a dog hookworm under her skin and it sort of crawled around on her foot for a couple of days, under the skin. Nothing came of it though, although we thought the worst would happen.

However, it is true that there are snakes and scorpions in the area. We have seen a number of snakes, and one scorpion, dead, but that's all. You get "sort" of used to these things. It's certainly not nearly as dangerous as car accidents at home, at least statistical-wise.

We brought quite a few of our basic toys for the children, and I have never been sorry. We brought puzzles, dolls, crayons, peg sets, a few games, records (must use portable record player which we got here), "bolts & nuts," Tinker Toys, etc. We also brought our tricycle, and bought another one from

Anne Harnish, playing with Swedish child. Sometimes the shoes just came off.

another missionary in Nairobi. I don't know if we will take it home though, as it has seen much hard use by now, but may try to sell it here. We brought many children's books. We brought crayons, paints and scissors, although probably you could get them here. Two things I have had trouble getting are construction paper and **good** glue. Although a lot of these things might be available in the bigger cities, here you hardly ever get there to get them.

Another thing our children have just loved are these felt-tipped markers. Bring a good supply! Since we have subscribed to the Calvert School ever since we were here, first kindergarten, then First Grade, we have not lacked in paper (newsprint-type) or pencils or this kind of thing, and I don't know if they are available here or not. Pencils are, of course. I hope this has been helpful on toys. Favorite toys and basic toys I would certainly bring. Even though things are available here, the allowance doesn't always permit you to buy them, but you know all about that since you are just coming out of medical school.

About food. Milk you can buy at the door locally, and you can also get just about any kind of dried milk at the grocery stores. We use both. The milk from the local cows isn't Guernsey milk, if you know what I mean. You get very little cream, but if you buy a fairly lot you do get some nice cream for whipped cream, and Mrs. L. even makes butter sometimes. (They get a lot since they have so many children.) It is a little different than buying milk at the store—first you **strain** it (through a cloth or milk strainer), then you **pasteurize** it (but I **boil** it). Then, after you put it in the refrigerator overnight, skim off the cream, unless you want it in, and you have good skimmed milk. However, Dave has not been able to bring himself to drink it, although I myself do, and the children do some, when they don't hear us discuss it! I use it for cooking too. We also use a lot of whole dried milk which we get in about two gallon tin containers and mix with our boiled water. We boil our water, and filter it. You will need to buy a filter when you buy your household equipment. It's much cheaper to buy the milk at the door, to continue with that.

We have planted a garden each year. So far we have gotten a **little** lettuce, some red-beets, some carrots, and this year some green beans and some tomatoes. However, we have planted much! We have all sorts of trouble—poor soil, too many bugs, other people's chickens and turkeys eating our plants.

However, each year, we plant and plant and plant. Certainly it is an education for the children, if nothing else, and the children love to help their father who loves to farm. They especially have loved planting beans, because they come up so nicely! I must say, if you put a lot of time and planning and water into your garden, it will succeed no doubt. The German nurse who is here usually has a lovely garden. I wouldn't hazard a guess as to how much money it actually saves though! I suspect we have almost put more into seeds than we have gotten out of it. Dave really hasn't the time to care for it properly although he'd love to, and it costs too much for a garden boy, although some of the others do have them. Also, we have animals-again I would say more as a hobby than a money saver. We have chickens, ducks, turkeys, rabbbits, two cats, and two dogs! How's that for a little farm? We have eaten some of the rabbits and they're quite good, and it is certainly nice to have your own fresh eggs. At the door you can, at certain seasons at least, buy more eggs. You will soon learn to test an egg for freshness, put it in a pan of water. If it floats, don't buy it! I have found few like that however.

David and Marie Harnish with ducks.

We have a very large kitchen, and a very large pantry. Cupboard space is quite adequate. We have a gas two-burner plate with bottled gas, but I don't use it an awful lot. We usually cook with a wood stove and after you get used to it, and know the tricks your oven is up to, you rather like it. It has such a lovely huge cooking surface, and ranges from very hot to just warm to keep foods hot, and it does have its advantages.

Of course, you have to keep putting wood into it, and getting it started has been one of my problems but usually our house-girl, Bahtletti, does that for me first thing in the morning. She also carries in the wood. I do most of the cooking, although she helps me out when there is time. With our family of five, she is busy cleaning and washing (by hand). There are two washing machines here in the **hospital**. And, she washes the dishes usually. I have taught her to bake our bread, and she does well, as well as a few cakes. I would like to teach her more too, as much for her own knowledge as to help me. All of the people here have cooks but us, but I find this no burden.

We buy meat at the door, about 17 cents a pound, and although it's a bit tough, you can do most anything with it. We often use it as hamburgers (you need a meat grinder), the children love curry, and sometimes even as a roast, although I usually make it well done. A meat thermometer is good. You can get chickens sometimes. Once we had pork, and you can buy things like ham and sausage in the stores, although they are much more expensive. You can get cabbage, carrots, and potatoes the year round at the stores, as well as rice. You can buy anything tinned, again more expensive than in the U.S. You can get Corn Flakes, Rice Krispies, etc., but here they cost about 2-1/2 times as much. We eat a lot of oatmeal, Cream of Wheat, pancakes, and our favorite is eggs and toast when we have the eggs. We often have lemon juice from our

David Harnish washing dishes at home.

own trees, and mangoes, guavas, passion fruit, and sometimes bananas and oranges. All of these fruits are available here or nearby, very cheap in season; we have been surprised that it is only in season that we can get some of the things. This is not really a lush fruit-growing area. Bananas in season cost as little as 20 to 28 cents for an entire stalk.

We have a kerosene refrigerator which works well if you don't forget to fill it, but which always seems to need defrosting (but never is). We have electricity every morning until noon, and from 6:00 in the evening and all night. If you plan to use electrical appliances, it would probably pay to buy them here or in Europe, since the current is not the same. We had our children's record player with us, but even with a transformer, it didn't work right, and for this reason we bought one here. One thing I have missed because I used it so much, is an electric mixer. Actually, I have no electrical appliances here at all. However, an iron is something I wish I would have bought when we bought our household goods with the allowance TAP gives you. I iron (rather, Bahtletti does) with stove heated irons, and she does a good job, although I often wish I had an iron. It was my fault. Don't forget an ironing board, and also, a pressure cooker is invaluable, as well as a frying pan with a lid. We didn't get a lid for ours and I really miss one! If there's something you're really dependent on in your kitchen, do bring it! I wish I would have brought my food mill, because we just love guava sauce, and it is such a chore putting it through a sieve.

Folding sheets in our kitchen at Ilembula - note kerosene refrigerator in rear.

The children love it here. They have playmates all day long, something they did not have in Philadelphia. They all three speak a very adequate

Swahili by now, and even some Swedish, and a few words of the tribal language, Kibena, come out now and then. Nothing delights them more than to say something that we can't understand. A switch from where the parents talk one language so the children can't understand it! They can count fluently in Swedish. Anne, at 2-1/2 years, speaks English and Swahili quite well. It took the other two nearly a year to really get started speaking it, but she has the advantage of learning the language here from the beginning.

Hope this answers a few of your questions. Don't hesitate to write again. Seems like I can't get stopped once I get started. I had so many questions myself before I came that I know how you feel.

Will you be doing any traveling before you get here? We stayed a week at Shirati, where Dave has two aunts living. When you get here, you will probably eat with us until you feel that you can strike out on your own.

We bought most of our equipment in Nairobi, but we think now we would try to get it locally.

Love,
Flo

June 4, 1969
Ilembula, Tanzania

Dear Hersheys,   Just keep the pictures–

We got your very exciting letter yesterday—all about that concert. What wonderful reviews you are getting these days Hiram!!!!

Next time, don't be so "stiff" (whatever that means) and they won't have a thing to say about it. How sorry we are to be missing all of these wonderful concerts. Where do you all go afterwards? Do you just all go home? When we get back, maybe we can change that. Don't know how long we'll stay in the city though. Congratulations and how proud we are of you. Also, business must be good. New location!

Now, to thank you Janie, for that box of paints, paper, and supplies! It came week before last, and I have already used the things to make a picture of an African child, and to paint, a herd of elephants—from a picture, however. I could just paint all day . . . no time. I had brought my old paints along, but some of them are pretty well dried up and used, so what a wonderful thing to get these paints.

I must say, you have managed to make us feel not one bit neglected over here!! Thank you so much. The children continue to enjoy the things you have sent them too. They play with those boats in the bathtub every night nearly.

I would say the one outstanding thing that you have sent to them were those felt-tipped water colors. They loved them, and many of them have been all used up for some time now. I am wondering if you could send us another box of them, since you asked, and Mrs. L. would like if you could include a box for their children, which she would like to buy. Their children helped use ours as well. They make such wonderful primary colors. For days after we got that other box from you, Marie did nothing but stay in the house and paint. She made some very pretty things, but I never did send you anything like I promised, did I?

(Ilembula) Harnish children bathing - cold running water in tap.

About who might like magazines. There are probably other TAP couples who would appreciate magazines like I did, and there is one couple in particular, the Lowell Detweilers, who arrived in December, who may be interested. Their address is Box 198, Kahororo Secondary School, Bukoba, Tanzania. I have not asked them about this, but will, since I am writing them a letter today. They have a daughter Marie's age, and a son, 3, and I think lost a baby too if I heard correctly. They plan to visit us at the end of this month, and I must say, we look forward to it. Marie and Cheryl were inseparable last year at TAP retreat. The Detweilers graduated from Goshen.

If you have not already sent material for my sewing class, perhaps you could wait for the time being. I got some from Dar es Salaam through Harold Miller and the Christian Council of Tanzania, very cheap—mill ends and pieces with flaws. Some of the brighter colors (they are all plaids) the women are very fond of, but to my surprise, some of the material is traditionally worn here by the old men (as wrap around type) and they are not one bit interested in these! I, myself, think them quite pretty, and have in fact made curtains from some of this type that I bought in the local *duka* (store). However, if you have already sent the things (material), the women will be most delighted.

One problem with the local cloth, it is relatively heavy, limp, and ravels terribly. But still, I would like them to use what is available locally, and see that it can be very attractive as gowns, and not just as "wrap-arounds," although I have no real objection to these wrap-arounds either, and they are quite pretty. I have discovered that they are interested mostly in the type of dress that has a bodice and a gathered skirt—even for their infants. It would be so much simpler to sew these little easy gowns that hang from the shoulders, and which **I** prefer. They don't like the narrowness and shortness of the shifts (I guess that's the reason). As a matter of fact, the government has outlawed short skirts, along with football, wigs, and tight pants for men (western influence)!

I never heard how your part in the PTA play went off. And how is the Jefferson clinic bit doing? I have a friend on 4th Street, and the others on Elfreth's Alley, if you ever need to stay on in town. Just mention my name! (Jill C., 411 S. 4th – husband is an architect).

Don't let me forget to mention that the children are crazy about those records. We **all** know a lot of the tunes now, and for a while heard nothing but those two records! Incidentally, I don't think I ever heard a more blood thirsty record than that one about the 12 brothers, except maybe a few Bible stories.

The children are out gathering seeds or nuts or something from some trees—ours and L. A year ago I would have cautioned them about snakes, but it sort of goes in one ear and out the other these days! After all, they say, nothing has happened yet! I am living with it a bit more easily, I think sometimes, although I did get terribly upset again when we had those little green ones in the house again! Five, this year. They hatch out up in the attic someplace, I suppose. We haven't seen any for a couple of weeks now, maybe it's over for this year, but I still walk around watching my feet. They're picking up a good bit of Swedish.

Children playing in trees.

We took a couple of safaris lately with Dave. Nothing delights David more

Anne Harnish playing with these animals while on a trip.

than to go with Daddy in the LandRover, Marie too, for that matter. And on this trip to Iringa, we got to stay in the White Horse Inn, which was a wonderful treat for **me**. Also, on one of the safaris, we stayed with some American missionaries in Chimala, so that was nice too. They are great hunters; trophies all over the place; like a museum. Are you sure you can't come over and go hunting, Hiram? Dave wants to, at least once.

L to R: 2 Swedish missionary children, David and Marie Harnish. Trying to grind some cassava.

Love,
Flo

June 23, 1969
Ilembula, Tanzania

Dear Janie,

Two very nice things have happed to me since I last wrote to
you for which you are responsible. The first, I received that
book by Goertzel and Goertzel: *Cradles of Eminence*, and
the other I received a packet of magazines from you. Thank
you so much. *Cradles of Eminence* was great! I couldn't stop
reading it until I had it finished. It is certainly "reassuring"
on many points, **which** points I will discuss with you perhaps at some future time when we see each other. I'm sure
you don't have the slightest idea what I meant by that last
sentence, but let it pass.

Suffice it to say, I thought that the book was marvelous, and I
am grateful to have read it. The reason I thought it might be
applicable to me now, was that I had read a reference to the
book in Miriam Sieber Lind's *Around The Corner* (or whatever her column is called nowadays), in which she said that
if she had read the book when her children were younger,
perhaps she would not have tried so hard. Well, anything I
can read that makes me not try so hard is for me! However,
I am not sure it will have that effect on me, but perhaps the
opposite! Anyway, you went and **bought** the book and **sent**
it to me, instead of just reading it as a library book and pass-
ing on your opinion. A true friend. As to the magazines–I am
enjoying them fully. Can't get my work done!

This past weekend, Dave finally went game hunting. Not
exactly big-game hunting, and yet not exactly hunting either.
He went along on a hunting safari, and took pictures. He left
Saturday morning intending to come back Saturday evening.
Well, he didn't come back until Sunday afternoon. The first
day they saw some nice animals (topis, a gazelle-like animal), but their LandRover got stuck in the mud and they got

away. So, they decided to go again the next day, and so got up at 2:30 A.M. Sunday and went again. They got 4 topies, and they gave one to Dave, as well as the horns of another one. He came home with four quarters, so we set up a butcher shop in our laundry, and cut everything up into pieces. Then Dave put it (the meat) in the hospital freezer. Should be enough meat to last us at least for a month or two. It is much more tender than the local cow we buy. We had some today as a roast, and it was very good.

Dave is speculating on whether he ought to buy a gun and get a hunting license. They saw many elephants, but no zebra. He had wanted to get a zebra skin. However, the topi skin is quite nice too. Don't know if we will be able to get it out of the country. He is also trying to fix the head so it can be mounted along with the horns. It was quite an experience, but Dave was absolutely exhausted! As for me, I am quite satisfied hearing about it and have no desire to go myself.

The children were having a ball today watching the old man who is drying the skin and taking the meat from the head and tail. I thought this particular man had such a kind face and mentioned this fact to one of the other missionaries. Of course, then she had to tell me a lot of stuff about how he used to be when he was young, had children all over the place, etc., etc., etc! Why must someone always be disillusioning me? Before she told me this, I had given this "poor old man" a couple of guavas and a large cup of tea—the way they usually drink it—very strong, with lots of milk and sugar in it all boiled together. Some people can never say anything good about anybody else!

Our David is a real bug collector. No little bug escapes his beetle eyes. David is always coming in with a butterfly or something for Dave to put in his collection. What I would like to ask you, do you know the proper way to catch and preserve butterflies

Swedish missionary children watching a man butchering a topi head.

without damaging them? He always carries them in his grubby little paws, and they are already hurt by the time we see them. Seems like I recall you people were doing something with butterflies at one time, right? If you don't know off-hand, never mind. We will wait until we get back.

The children are also collecting rocks, stamps, and napkins. I was never much of a collector (for instance, salt and pepper shakers make me absolutely nauseated.) (By the way, do you have a salt and pepper shaker collection?), but the stamps are now a family project here. I have to collect them if I want to or not, because they are brought to me in great eagerness. It is really rather interesting, I must admit. We also have a very tiny coin collection, that we hope to add to on our way home.

So much for what we're doing. What are you doing? Are you taking any summer courses? After you are a midwife (?) will you practice? I just read that article in one of the magazines you sent about the father participating in the delivery—Lamaze method, I think. I must confess, I am more interested in hearing the mother's opinions, and especially those having their third babies as that article said. Not all women (I would venture to say, very few women) have a husband as interested as he was—a pity, say I.

Enough rambling. I would be delighted to hear from you soon.

Love, Flo

P.S. Did I tell you what David said one time when he saw some writing (or scribbling, I guess) in one of the magazines you sent? He thought it must have been that "little boy" that lives at your house—meaning Jimmy! Our Anne now speaks in 8-10 word sentences (in English of course), knows all her colors and seems to be getting quite grown up. The other day she said, "I like peoples!" I thought it rather philosophical for a 2-1/2 year old. Bragging again, I am.

June 24, 1969
Ilembula, Tanzania

Dear Janie,

I just received your letter today, even before my last one was sealed, but I see that I don't even have space to scribble in the margins. I forgive you gladly for not writing oftener, although even in saying that I wish you would write oftener and I look forward to your letters very much. Amongst those people that are friends, we write and hear from you more often than anyone else! Even our families, except for both sets of parents, don't write very often! But, we keep getting things from you and that's just like a letter, almost. As to the material that you sent, you have been most generous, and I hope I can use it wisely. Things have been coming through in two to four months lately, so let's hope there is no dock strike!

About Jimmy, I can see how you can brag about his latest feat—believe me, I would too. I don't see how a parent can help bragging now and then! I am glad for him and you, even though it strikes up a bit of envy! As to bragging about David, I think I did that already with his early singing, didn't I? More bragging, David can also speak one language fluently: English, and another quite well: Swahili, and smatterings of a third one: Swedish. The same is true for the other two of course. (The L. children speak both Swedish and Swahili fluently, and English fairly well. Some even have smatterings of Kibena!)

Marie has also learned to ride a two-wheeler. For about two weeks, more or less, the L. had their two-wheeler repaired. Their 6 year old and our Marie both learned to ride it during that period of time amidst **much** quarrelling as to whose turn it was. We ourselves have only one of those large English-type tricycles, which seems to satisfy David's desires at the moment. Actually, since the L.'s two two-wheelers are out of commission, ours sits here too. We brought our small tricycle along for Anne, but so far she used it as a Kiddy Kar. I think maybe the other two were riding it by this age, although I'm not too sure about that. I know David did it earlier than Marie, which I attributed to his longer legs in part. (See below for date—Anne now rides her tricycle very nicely!)

Marie is out of school now, as of this week, and has just in the last weeks discovered that she can read all of those early-reader Suess books with great speed. Earlier she had tried, and had indeed read some, with some difficulty, and with my help. Suddenly she can read them, and she's delighted. The last couple of days of school I let her choose what she wanted to, and that's when she discovered it. She brought three books, and asked me if she could read all those. David has started to learn to read too, by his own request. It really started this way . . . I have started Marie on a soprano recorder which she is supposed to practice every day after lunch. David wanted to do something too, so first, just to give him something to do, he printed his name. He learned that in about two days, and from there we went to numbers, and he soon did that, then we went to the letters and a little reading. I must confess to being a bit guilty about spending as much time with him along these lines as I did with Marie.

We got a letter from MCC asking us to come back for another term. Mixed reactions from us. Keep this on the Q.T.–Doubt if we will.

Believe it or not, it is now the **13th of August**!

I just reread what I read until now—drivel, all of it. But, guess I'll go on. That material, it arrived about the 11th or 12th of July. It is really wonderful. Thank you, thank you. I can't remember, but think I mentioned it in Hiram's letter from Dave. I was so delighted to see it, and the scissors, thread, needles, and other things. We are just now finishing up the other materials I got from Harold Miller. It went much faster than I anticipated, so the timing is just perfect. Actually, that other material went (in part) without the kind of supervision I wanted to give.

With yours, I am going to be very strict. By this I mean, I am going to hand it out one piece at a time, help with that, and then only, will I start on a new piece. Did I tell you that I am charging a little bit for each piece they sew? This I am doing by their request, and it enables us to buy elastic (oh yes, thanks for your wonderful strong elastic), hooks and eyes, etc. I even bought a couple of scissors (one of which has **disappeared**), and our present goal is a hand operated sewing machine. We are over half-way to this goal. When I see you sometime I will tell you of all of my experiences with this group. It is a bit different than working with a church group at home. Last week I had tea for everyone, and bread (which they love), and gave a little talk, Zachaeus and his change of heart and return of stolen things after he met Jesus. (My Swahili is improving slowly, but must admit I read most of it.) Now I am toying with the idea of having lectures on health and family planning, with skits to follow. Probably just all ideas, and will come to nothing!

Please, again, thanks so much for the books and coloring books. The children **love** them, and that *Hansel and Gretel* is **beautiful**. (What a wicked stepmother though!)

We spent a week at Matema. The water was cleanest I have ever seen, and for the first time we **swam** here. I wish I could send you one of their pots, and I may try again—they are so lovely. Mosquitoes 90% infected with malaria, so we hastened under our nets each night. However, we read *TIME*'s cover story on nudity there, and it certainly made interesting reading in that context! We were the only ones with bathing suits—also the only ones staring or being stared at. We saw our first skirts made of banana leaves—only one or two though. Most had clothes on out of the water.

Love, Flo

July 15, 1969
Ilembula, Tanzania

Dear Mrs. Detuerk,

Imagine our great surprise and delight to receive a wonderful box of "goodies" from you last week! How very thoughtful of you. The children were beside themselves with joy seeing that good candy! We can get good candy here, but on our budget we usually don't.

And I can't say how pleased I was to get all those "luxury" items for the kitchen. Please accept our sincere thanks! I used that stroganoff mix for some guests we had this week, and it really was delicious. Do you use it a lot? I looked up in my cookbook, *Joy of Cooking*, what was actually in a stroganoff and I think the package mix had a lot more than the cookbook asks for. We certainly enjoyed it.

About two weeks or so ago, Dave finally got to go hunting, although he didn't actually shoot anything except with his camera. The people he went with live on the edge of the great Ruaha area which contains many of the wild animals usually thought to inhabit every place in Africa. They are a tribe which originally came from someplace close to Pakistan, and are known as Baluchis, and often come here as patients. They killed a topi, which is a large gazelle-type animal, with delicious meat. It's actually what I made the stroganoff with. The meat from the animals one shoots here is usually much more tender than the local "cow" we buy at the door, for reasons that I can't explain.

Child watching man salvaging skin from topi head. Dave went hunting with Beluchi people. He did not shoot the topi, but it was given to him.

On that hunting safari they saw many elephants, but no zebras, which is what Dave had really hoped to get—for the skin. Guess if we want a zebra skin, we'll have to buy it, although the topi skin is quite nice too, sort of a rust brown with large black spots in it. We tried to have the head and horns mounted, but it got too buggy and smelly, so finally Dave just saved the antlers themselves. He spent a night in the LandRover, got stuck in the mud, cooked over an open fire from the freshly killed animal, and all in all had enough troubles to make the trip exciting, but not dangerous.

As for me, I am leading my usual life. I do the cooking, but have taught our household help the bread-making, and at this point she does it better than I do. I have even taught her how to make your banana bread, so who knows where that recipe will end up! She also helps some with the cooking, but there is not much time after she does cleaning, washing (by hand), and ironing.

Right now I feel relatively free since I have given the children a summer vacation from school, but it will resume again in September. I am teaching by the Calvert Correspondence course, and will have a second grader and a kindergartner. I don't know what we'll do about schools when we get back to Elfreth's Alley next year, there in the heart of the city, but I do worry about it a bit. Guess I'll have to go to school with them every day. You can't send such young children by themselves across the busy streets.

I also have a sewing class, in which I am (trying) to teach some of the women of the church to sew. I spend quite a bit of time with this, and it is the only thing I do that can be called a missionary endeavor in the classic sense of the word at least. They sew by hand, so the first thing I do is give them a needle (!) and show them how to hold a scissors properly. However, some of them do quite well, and I must admit, I am a bit surprised. Others, well . . .

Tomorrow we hope to take about a week's vacation and go to a lake, Matema, and go swimming. We have not gone swimming yet here because most of the rivers and lakes are just loaded with Bilharzia. They say that Matema is not, so we will go, and I know the children will like it, as will we. It is an area that is warmer than here, with many mosquitoes and malaria, so I plan to take along our mosquito nets,

> We usually did not swim because we were afraid of getting *bilharzia*, caused by a liver fluke—a bad disease!

and plenty of insecticide. Also, whenever you go anywhere here, unless you are staying with friends or in a Guest House, you take **everything** with you, including drinking water and food.

The children, now 7, 5, and 3, are certainly enjoying life here. They are pretty competent in Swahili now, and picking up a lot of Swedish from their little Swedish missionary friends, with whom they play much. They play a lot with the local clay, which they get right out of the ground, make things, and then "fire" them in our fireplace at night.

These days, we usually have a fire in the evenings, but I suppose you have your air-conditioner turned on! The climate here is very ideal we think, and you never do experience that sultry humid weather that is so intolerable. It is due to the fact that we are in the

Harnish and Swedish missionary children at the river. David 4th from left; Anne 5th from left; Marie, 7th from left.

mountains. Coming back to the clay, it is what the local people make their cooking pots out of, with a rounded bottom, which is then set over three stones for cooking. It looks a little like the flower pots in the States, but has many more impurities in it.

Thank you again for thinking of us in that most delightful way!

Sincerely,
Flo

LETTERS

1969

From Dave to Hiram

August 1, 1969
Ilembula, Tanzania

Dear Hiram,

I'm glad you and the family had another enjoyable time at Cape Cod. It brings back memories of the week(s) we spent with you there, and the women catching those huge dogfish which we threw back.

We spent a week at Lake Malawi, between Tanzania and Malawi, about 200 miles from Ilembula. It is a beautiful clear fresh warm water lake, so we went swimming morning and afternoons. There, the Africans bathe too, and play in the sand in the same suits they were born with. They also do fishing and have boats dug out of tree trunks. Some Baptist, Lutheran, and Catholic missions dot the beaches of this huge lake. Some of the missions have powered motor boats. At certain times of the

On vacation to Lake Matema. Old German built house Harnishes stayed in. First landing on moon took place while we were here.

year it is inaccessible except by boat.

These are quite exciting days with the Americans landing on the moon. It is really hard to believe. The precision and flawless rockets are amazing. Also amazing is that much of the world is also excited by the event. Other missionaries of Europe sat glued to their radios and those Africans who are educated were also quite excited. Now, the Voice Of America (radio) has offered free pictures of the astronauts and the moon to non-U.S. citizens. Some of our staff have sent for them. This seems to me to be the best thing the U.S. has done for the world in the past years, and also good for international good will. This event should not backfire.

Unfortunately, our radio (which last year was stolen) is now in the repair shop so that we got the moon shot only in news summary. During those days all radio news was about the moon. The boss of the radio shop where we had taken our radio to be fixed died, and a few weeks ago when we had tried to get it out we weren't able to. That radio has been bad luck all along.

I was just reading today's news that Sen. Kennedy attended the funeral of the secretary (*i.e., The Standard* out of Dar es Salaam) at Plymouth, Pa. Did you attend the funeral too, since it is so near to Harleysville? The article also stated that he has not been of good character since Robert's death, with much drinking, fast driving, possible divorce and company with other girls. Is this really true?

Our news is really rather local since *Time* magazine has not come since June. I think MCC has forgotten to renew the subscription. We miss **all** the moon stuff.

I see that business is booming, but stocks are down. I hope Georgia Pacific Systems, Capital Chemway, and U. C. do go up so as to make some profit. I saw that IBM bounced up to 335 which is heartening. Also, Merck has hit 90 recently. I believe you bought some in 1967 at around 70. I really have no suggestions for any change in stocks at present.

The Lowell Detweiler family of Bukoba (on Lake Victoria) visited us for five days the beginning of July, which we enjoyed. Also, while we were at Lake Malawi, some hunter friends brought me a zebra so I am busy trying to prepare the hide to bring back to America. We heard today that Mrs. Clyde Shenk, missionary from Musoma-Shirati area, was killed last week in an airplane accident. They were from Willow Street (my home congregation). We also met them several times here, and two of their children were, or are, in TAP. We don't know any details, but are saddened by this tragedy.

There seem to be robbers loose in this area during the past six months; hospitals and missionaries seem the prime targets. Several people (not missionaries) have been killed, and several injured. A Swedish missionary's house, two houses away, was robbed at night three weeks ago. A Swedish friend of ours was robbed at knife-point at Bulongwa, in a home we have visited in and ate in many times. We ourselves have not been disturbed.

We are all in good health, except for colds, and working as usual.

Sincerely,
David

P.S. from Flo. Please tell Janie that some coloring books have arrived for the children, plus two pocket books for me (both read and enjoyed already!) and that we are all delighted and thankful. We never have to pay customs on books, either, so this is an added bonus. Also, the cloth for the women who sew has come and I am truly grateful, and so are they! I will write soon. I don't know if you know how much your continued support means to us, but many of our other friends seem far away, but not you two!

LETTERS

1969

From Flo to Janie

September 24, 1969
Ilembula, Tanzania

Dear Janie,

The whole family has gone off happily in the LandRover to
Njombe but me, so I will try to write to you and a few other people that I haven't written to for an age. (Like my poor parents!
Mom writes so faithfully, but me!!) First, let me thank you for
the paints and the material, which arrived the week before last.
The children are **very** delighted, albeit I have put it away until
our next safari to Nairobi in December. Mrs. L. is happy with
the set, and I would like to ask you how much the sets were,
because we "ordered" these from you. I couldn't tell from the
label, but from the other time I thought they were someplace
between $3.00 and $4.00. She has given me some money, but
I will wait until I hear from you about the exact amount.

The material is very pretty. Did I describe the scene where I gave out some of your material? The women couldn't get down to cutting and sewing because they were so busy admiring it! One held one end, another held the other end of a couple of pieces, and they just stood there ooohing, and aaahing. They are **so** happy with this material. I sometimes wonder if I am really teaching much **sewing**, but they do have to sew and cut it themselves, so I guess it does accomplish something. The dresses you can buy in the local stores here are all cut sleeveless, with a fairly low neck, and no opening of any kind, which means that very shortly they are torn, one reason being because of the necessity of nursing the babies constantly.

I'll go through your letters now. The first one I picked up is dated June 15. Maybe I did write since then. The first paragraph asks about Mr. George, the African we had asked about, who was admitted to Augustana. He is still here, and still trying to find someone to support him. The church here has refused to sponsor him, for various and sundry reasons. He does have some promises of help during his last several years there. He is still working on it, and we hope he is successful on his own in trying to get the money. Thank you for your offer of trying to collect money for him—if Dave thinks there is good reason to go ahead with trying to collect this money, we will let you know. At the moment, just let it rest unless of course you would hear of someone who really is eager to do this kind of thing. He has recently gotten married, to a nurse, I have no idea if he would plan to take her along or not.

Mr. George was very persistent and ended up being a urologist! He visited us in Ephrata in 2005!

About duty on the boxes we have received. We have paid duty on nearly everything we have received, with the exception of books, magazines, and records. Also, the material that went through Harold Miller in Dar did not require any, since it is to be used for the local people here.

As for what to send us for Christmas–I have somewhat purposely omitted saying anything. We are thinking in terms of coming home now, and think perhaps it would be better to wait until we get home to accumulate anything more that has to be brought along. I might make one suggestion though, that would include all three children, and that is a record I saw advertised in *Grade Teacher*, October, 1968, p. 88. The record is "Frank Luther Sings Lois Lenski Songs." It says to order direct from the publisher: Henry Z. Walck, Inc., 19A Union Square West, New York, N.Y. 10003. (It is cheaper for teachers and schools–do you or I qualify?) As for me, just send me the money??? This is what I would like—I have an almost constant parade of people at the door asking for work.

We feel on our MCC budget we can afford and need one person to help out, but some of these people really need work. It is work they want, not a handout. So, if instead of sending me a Christmas present, you could just send one or two dollars, indirectly I would get a very nice present of a lovely green, weedless, garden and lawn, by letting some of the more needy looking ones pull a few weeds for an hour or so. The prevailing wage is about 8 cents an hour (in American terms) so a little would go a long way you see. Or maybe I could buy some little health booklets especially on feeding of children that I encountered, and give these to my sewing class. I did order them already as a matter of fact, and Dave said the hospital could pay for them but I then couldn't have all of them. They too cost about 8 cents apiece. You wouldn't believe that people couldn't get 8 cents would you? Actually, I suppose most of them could get it, at least in our area, but I doubt if their system of priorities would suggest that they buy a health pamphlet.

I actually believe though, that some of these people don't even have enough money to buy salt for their food! I suppose there is very little to be accomplished by **giving** them money, except it certainly is sharing on the part of those who have it. (I once suggested this in one of our Bible studies here among the missionaries, and was promptly hooted down!) Sometimes I must confess that I even wonder what good it is giving them such false standards as new clothes, such as maybe I am doing!

I wonder if God really intended for people to wear clothes in a climate such as this, and like in Dar es Salaam where it's really steamy! What do you think? One thing that I think we can and must share with them is our knowledge of the factors that cause sickness. Hooray for Dave. But, to get good food, *i.e.*, meat, and eggs, it does take money. I always get off on these tangents instead of just writing a simple letter about what we had for dinner today, and the cute things the children are saying.

To continue about Christmas presents—Dave says he doesn't want anything now, but maybe when he comes home!!!! Now—what do you people want? Drums? Local material? Baskets? Carvings? ??? Snake skins? Please say!

How I wish we could see your baby. She won't seem real to us until we see her I suppose. How are you doing by now on the baby bottle bit? I can imagine she is quite the center of attraction in your household these days. Have you quite given up your midwifery goal? (I hope not.) Now that Art Kennels are closer, do you see them much? I got a letter from Louise Hogge yesterday—she seems quite happy and contented.

We just yesterday got our first issue of *Time* again for ages (we're supposed to be getting it continuously, but we think MCC goofed) and guess who's in it? Our own Myron Augsburger! (Wouldn't he be surprised if he'd see that statement, since he doesn't know me from Adam!) Also glad to see those miniskirts and maxiskirts! Me, in a miniskirt?

I'm back at teaching school again. Takes up all of my mornings. Even Anne comes and wants me to help her do "school work." I don't know how the old classroom teachers did it (I mean the one-room schools) because all three of the children want my attention at the same time. Marie is beginning to enjoy reading quite a bit and is discovering the books and stories herself now. We are in the midst of telling time, and what seems so easy to me, seems difficult for her. I guess she is getting it now, but I don't think she is a "born" time teller. The math books I think are geared to the so-called "new math" and in some ways I think it is more difficult. Maybe just because it's difficult for me! Much of the material seems redundant, and a whole new vocabulary must be learned. It is said that the end results, rather, objectives, are the same. Have you any opinion on this matter?

I can't think of anything else much to say just now, so will stop. Don't forget to tell me what those paints cost!

Afternoon now, and I haven't done **anything**. Absolutely wonderful day!

Love, Flo

P.S. Oh yes, we made a tape with some slides the other night. I think Dave is sending it today. I wanted to fill up the rest of the tape with chatter, but Dave said it had to go. Definitely amateurish, but we enjoyed making it and I hope you enjoy it too. It can be passed on to parents and **close** (only) friends.

Incidentally–I think that "Baby Sue" doll you sent Anne last Christmas is the most-bathed doll in Africa . . . 2 or 3 times a day! Her eyes are getting rusty.

October 13, 1969
Ilembula

Dear Janie,

I keep wondering if you got the tape and the slides. That was
a very funny letter attached to it. What it means is this–after
you've looked at them, send them to Dave's parents at Lancaster, and they can send them on to my parents in Indiana,
and they will send them back to you. It might be after you
get them back and are through with them, the Kirchners in
Philadelphia might be interested.

And now to answer your letter. That little Beth is really cute!
She looks very alert on that picture of her and Peter, and
Peter looks so proud of her. Must admit to a twinge of envy
here. She is really really sweet. And you are nursing her!
Unbelievable. I have been telling everyone
here, and they just don't want to believe it.

Beth was an adopted baby.

Then I tell them that I have known you for
over twenty years (yes, really!) and that
you tell nothing but the truth. And I show them the picture of
Beth. Maybe together we will stage a revolution in breastfeeding. (Actually it's not needed so much here.) I certainly hope
you contemplate writing this up in journals and journals.

Changing the subject a bit, a British woman in her twenties,
married to an Italian—they are working on the Dar to Zambia road—just delivered an infant here last week. She had no
real difficulties as I understand it, but she has vowed to have
no more children, even though this was her third girl. (It was
a beautiful, eight pound baby.) She is breastfeeding it with
little difficulty, as she did her other two, and was astounded
to hear that in the States many women don't breastfeed
these days. What is the actual statistic do you know—women
who don't, *i.e.*? The women from Finland, Britain, Sweden,
and here all claim that nearly all of the women do breast-

feed their babies. I wonder if that's really true (or were they here too long) and if so, what in the world went wrong in the States? Too many men obstetricians? Most of those other women claim that there are many midwives in their respective countries and that doctors only see the women if there is trouble. I only know one midwife in the whole United States (the former Elnora Weaver, remember her?), although there are more. Is that still your goal? Maybe I'll have to join you! We'll set up a practice and take calls.

I feel for you in that Anatomy class. When I took Anatomy way back in Goshen, I didn't learn a thing! I realized it even more when years later, at Jefferson, I was supposed to teach a subject I didn't know anything about. I learned it then— what I know, that is. It's like learning a language. I have always maintained that the people (educators) who say do not memorize, have never taken an Anatomy course!

I should have known you would have sent Christmas presents if I didn't say anything, instead of just procrastinating, as I would have done! We are really **delighted** of course. Now, **please** don't send those other things I mentioned. Since I wrote to you, one of my sisters' (Lila) classes sent me some money for the work here, so I do have some now to work with. It came as a complete surprise, and I didn't even know they were contemplating it. If I need it for any other project, I will let you know. Do pray that I will use the money that was sent (fifty dollars) in a good way and that it will really meet a need here. It is not even from my home church, and I surely hope I can be a good instrument for the use of this money.

Do you have a chance to get to the library these days? If so, or maybe you know already, would you look up firing pottery, and whether it requires a terribly high heat to put a glaze on pots. What I specifically want to know is if the people here would be able to glaze their pots. They use dried

cow manure (?!) to fire them, but I have always wondered
what would happen if they glazed them. Also, how do these
glazes come? Powder? It's really a shame to waste their cow
manure by burning it when they should be putting it back on
their fields. They spend hours gathering the stuff, and one
sees big baskets of it. Probably a rather lively market for it,
although I haven't really investigated this. This cow manure
(I think) gives a slow long-burning heat, but we have successfully fired small pots in our fireplace. Marie does it all the
time. Just wondering. I did see some beautifully glazed pots
in Nairobi, which they claimed were made locally, but that's
far away in another country.

Are you **sure** you can't take a flying trip over here to see us
before we come home? How we'd love it!

Love, Flo

P.S. I thought I was at the bottom of the page! Dave went
to Iringa yesterday and is supposed to be back today some
time. Our car is in need of **major** repairs and has now been
in the garage for 6 weeks! He went to see if he can find out
what the score is. We will need it to go to TAP retreat in Nairobi. (Aren't you glad I type?)

LETTERS

1969

*First letter: Dave to Cecil and Margaret Ashley, in Brazil
Footnote by Flo.*

November 4, 1969
Ilembula, Tanzania

Dear Ashley's,

My thoughts were drawn to Brazil, you, and your tasks by
two incidents today, so I thought I had better write a letter.
This morning I had a few minutes so I picked up *Christian
Living*, July, 1969, and read Rosanna Hostetler's article,
"Sight Seeing For a Brazilian Christmas." She mentioned Sao
Paulo, Campinas, Brasilia, etc. That was the first thing. Then
tonight, the Swedish missionary gave me a 15 page outline
of the Lutheran World Federation for the Fifth Assembly in
Porto Alegre, Brazil, July 14-24, 1970. The World Conference
Program looks quite good, the theme being "Send Into the
World." Maybe some of you will be representatives. I noticed
in the article there were pros and cons about whether the

Ilembula Lutheran Hospital

Dave determining if patient can read better with donated glasses.

conference should be held in Brazil because of the political situation.

We have also heard of the changes in government, and of the kidnapping of Ambassador Elbrick. You have no doubt heard of the death of Senator Dirksen—one of my favorite senators. Do you subscribe to *Time*?

Tanzania at the moment is fairly peaceful, although we did hear of an unsuccessful coup on Zanzibar, with executions. Kenya is having tribal conflicts between the two dominant tribes. The lid seemed to blow off slightly when the economic Minister, Tom Mboya, was shot. TAP has many teachers in Kenya, as well as the headquarters for all of East Africa in Nairobi. We will have to wait to see the outcome.

I am quite busy at this 200 bed hospital, curing tropical diseases. There is much surgery too—cataract extractions, amebic liver abscesses, acute abdomen, c-sections, and ectopic pregnancies. Many days I don't feel much like a missionary in managing the hospital as the chronic problems are balancing the budget, keeping a well-trained staff, getting adequate drug supplies, and personnel complaints. (I am also the hospital administrator.) There are also court cases of patients which I must attend. Discipline to those workers who steal money and don't do their jobs well are among the problems. I didn't know that these problems would be included as part of being a medical missionary!

Overall, we enjoy working here and helping those who otherwise would not be helped. Also, we are not caught in the "keep up with the Jones'" race here in the desolate plains. We enjoy the big game parks—elephants, lions, giraffes, and snakes. (Enjoy?) In general we like participating in the work of these African churches. Most of the church work is actually done by Africans, so that our ministry is mainly to help those who are sick. I suppose Flo will add some more. We do think of your work in Brazil, and the church there in our prayers.

Sincerely, Dave

(Foot Note)
Dear Margaret, Cecil, and Marcos,

Dave's right, when I started typing this I was hoping there would be a space left for me. He wrote his letter at least two weeks ago, but I did not get around to typing it and doing my part until today. I wonder how you are, really. Whether you have been sick, what are you actually doing every day, whether you're nursing, teaching, etc? What is Marcos doing, going to school there? Are there any other children in your family? I remember him very well, especially his beautiful eyes and his very robust appearance, at, was it 4 years of age when you visited us in Philadelphia? I think he's just about Marie's age, right? She will be 8 in March of 1970.

We are in good health at the moment and have been for a long time. We have not had the bronchitis and other winter colds that we usually manage to get in Philadelphia. The African children seem to have many runny noses and we have had a few. I am teaching Marie by the Calvert Corre-

Anne being carried by Marie, and Swedish missionary child carrying her sister. This is the way the children played.

spondence system, and am enjoying it, especially when other things don't crowd in and take my time. David, who will be 6 in April next year, is taking the kindergarten work, but is also learning to read. Anne, who was just 3 in October is always begging me for "school work" too, and I do let her do something now and then, but I really don't have time to do it. Guess she will have to wait until we get to America and the other two go to school. They have all learned Swahili, as have we (we went to Language School for 3 months), and since they play nearly every day with Swedish missionary children, have also picked up quite a bit of Swedish, which we have not. Nothing delights them more than to say something that we can't understand. What a pity that they will probably lose it when we go home.

I am doing no nursing or teaching at all at the moment. I do the cooking (we do have one housegirl), Dave's typing, have a sewing class which meets once or twice a week here, and find I have a pretty full schedule. My heart has really gone out to the women here—it is a land of polygamy (although forbidden in Christian circles) and much hard work. Just now the thing that hurts me the most is seeing the women carry bricks (I figured out yesterday that is about 114 pounds) on their heads for a mile or so; when they get 100 bricks (6 to 7 at a load) in a pile they get a shilling and a half (21 cents in U.S. money.) Some have babies tied to their backs as well. But Dave says it is not the actual physical work that is bad but the diseases and poor nourishment. I'm also toying with the idea of health teaching—but the trouble is how can you tell them to eat fruit everyday if they don't have it and don't have money to buy it? They need an agriculturist here—and much rain. I could go on and on. We look forward to going back to Philadelphia (same place) with feelings of anticipation and dread. Will miss leaving here, but feel we should get the children into schools.

Love, Flo

(Below is what the children have to say, to Flo, remembering a bus trip from Dar es Salaam to Ilembula.)

9/18-19-20/1969
Dar es Salaam-
Bus ride to Ilembula-
I didn't sleep well.

I was always going to sleep and a big bump again and woke up again. Not so many bumps on the Dar es Salaam Road to here. Daddy didn't sleep well either and he fell down on me—the mosquito bite hurts. I was on the back seat—slept fine, but I kept on bouncing. (D.) Anne was right behind me. And I was right behind her. (D.) We had a good bus driver. Write that we waited and waited and thought the trucks were the buses and we couldn't tell which was the bus and finally the bus came. The trucks were on the road and we couldn't get past and we had to wait till they got off. You fell asleep and Daddy was going to take a picture but you woke up. We got in a Pugeot Taxi to come to Luther House. We ate eggs, cheese sandwiches, peanuts, chocolate. The *choos* (toilets) along the way were very stinky-better to go in the bush. Many people were on the bus. The men just go potty right along the road.

LETTERS

1970

January 1970
Ilembula, Tanzania

Dear Hershey Friends,

The reason you did not get Christmas Cards from us is because we were on "safari." Therefore, we send our greetings and best wishes at the beginning of this New Year, and hope that your lives will be enriched as you serve the Christ in your corner of this planet. We hope that we ourselves have given as much as we have received in the past year.

The biggest recent event in our lives was the big journey we took. We were headed for Nairobi to our annual TAP (Teachers Abroad Program) Retreat, but took the long way around Lake Victoria. First, we visited Williamson Diamond Mines—we saw real diamonds, then spent two days in Mwanza. We were pleased to see Aunts Mary and Elizabeth there, and spent a day with them. Then on to Bukoba to the home of fellow TAPPERS and on up to Kampala in Uganda.

At Kampala, Dave attended a 3-day Surgical Conference at modern Makerere Medical College, which could be the envy of any Medical School in the States. It is spacious, air-conditioned, has closed-circuit TV for lectures and is well staffed. There is none comparable in East Africa. NIH, Bethesda, MD has its own building there for cancer research, concentrating on lymphomas (for example, Burkitt's). The conference concerned surgical problems of the tropics such as VV fistulae, urethral strictures, cancers, polio, and leprosy rehabilitation.

Murchison Falls Game Reserve was our next 2-day stop. Its uniqueness lies in being located on the Nile River. Did you know that the Nile originates from Lake Victoria? We took a launch trip up the Nile to Murchison Falls and saw many crocodiles and hippos. The crocodiles were basking in the sun with their mouths open and flies crawling in their throats—this we saw from our launch of course. At Murchison Falls we discovered that we have gone a third of the distance from here to Cairo! All in all we traveled over 3,000 miles over washboard roads and ferries in our trusty VW (not always so trusty)!

In Nairobi we had a most stimulating 10-day retreat. Don Jacobs with his creative thinking and leadership certainly revitalized our spirits. There was much lively discussion as well as much lively physical activity—squash, tennis, etc. One of the problems that came into focus is that the white man is very much needed here for his skills and technical assistance, but he is really not very much wanted. We must live and work with love in this framework of thought. Perhaps we are called to absorb some of the hostility which has been engendered by former "colonialism."

We had our family Christmas here at Ilembula. The children were very excited about Christmas. David, 5, is trying to sort out the story of Santa Claus, but Marie, 7, seems to know. Marie is enjoying reading now, playing the recorder a bit, and

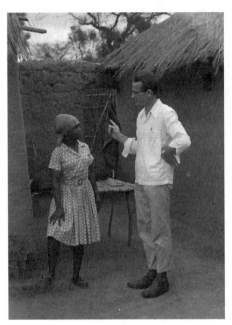

Dave giving instructions to Tanzanian woman.

Clockwise from right: Marie, Max (dog), David, Anne, Dave Harnish playing a game.

playing checkers and chess. David likes checkers as well as other games, and catching butterflies and other insects. He seems to have to shout sometimes, simply because shouting is necessary! Anne, 3, wants to do everything everyone else does. All three speak Swahili, and some Swedish.

The hospital is busy, and Dave copes with the daily list of surgical problems and administrative details. There have been over 500 major operations for the year past. The really difficult problems are corrective surgery in polio deformities, Vesico-vaginal fistuli, and cancers such as Kaposi's and Epithelioma of the skin. There are also weekly lectures and clinical rounds with the students to prepare them for their examinations.

Probably the next big event is our return to the States this summer. We would like to tour a bit of Europe on our way. We hope to arrive in Philadelphia in June, and look forward to seeing all of you. We would be delighted to hear from you. Our address in Philadelphia will be the same as it was before: 111 Elfreth's Alley, Philadelphia, PA 19106.

My current gripe here—I am so sick of the missionaries who complain that the local malnourished populace is stealing fruit from "their trees!" I just see red when I hear this discussed! Dave tells me to forget it but I can't! They should be **giving** them to the people, in my opinion. Oh, well. Some of these people have been here too long and now look upon this as their country.

Marie, Anne, David Harnish in Ilembula.

It's the rainy season here and we have had much rain, so Anne is busily watering flowers! Marie is bringing home mangoes, which I can't eat, and I'm not sure where David is playing at the moment. This morning I gave them a lecture about not just "playing" when their friends are working, but to help them work, usually hoeing the garden.

Love, Flo (added to by Dave)

P.S. I'm so sick of typing up these carbons with all their mistakes, but might as well send one to you. Surely I wrote more than a card to you! Didn't you get the one about the Christmas presents? If not, we were terribly, terribly pleased!

When Nd Umorem talks about rebel-held territory, I presume he means Ifo-held. Here in Tanzania, the Ifos were the heros.

Enjoyed your letter thoroughly and thanks for the enclosure—it came as a surprise to me.

January 5, 1970
Ilembula, Tanzania

Dear Janie,

First, let me thank you for those wonderful, wonderful presents which we are fully and thoroughly enjoying! To begin with Anne—we had play-dough all over the house for days, made by Anne and her siblings and all the L----- children. They loved it. And David's eyes nearly popped out of his head when he saw that big green truck, and those little cars are what he plays with by the hour. He's so pleased that the little hoods go up. And Marie, well so far she and her friends have made 10 of those potholders on that little loom! And you couldn't have pleased her more with that box of crayons. She certainly treasures it. Thank you for being somehow able to find presents that pleased the children so much!

As for us—I can't leave that Frommer book alone—we did have the old edition of it just before we came, but this is so timely. Honestly, when you read it you want to pack and go tomorrow. And that game—to see if you're a genius, you know—can't remember what it's called now—first time through I had 8 left! Dave claims it's what you do on the first time through that is the deciding factor, so you can see where that left me. Once, I got it down to two, however. We had a party here the Saturday after Christmas, and everyone was quite intrigued by it. No one had only one left however. Have you? We have read that most fascinating issue of *Life*. As for the material, since we had to pay customs on it, I think maybe I can use a little bit for us if that's O.K. with you. It certainly is lovely. I would like to make a dress for myself, and maybe one for Marie—we seem to be the ones needing clothes. There is no question of what to do with any material that is left or with the other pieces. The women are truly grateful I think. Thank you very, very much for your very, very thoughtful gifts. We really appreciate what must have been a tremendous effort shopping and packing these things.

We enjoyed your Christmas picture very much. Beth already has changed her appearance a great deal from her baby picture. It's a sweet picture. I remember Jimmy as having dark hair, but in that picture he looks so blond. Peter looks dark and Beth dark. Tommy looks like he has hair about the color of our three. It's so amazing when they were born Anne was dark, David light, and Marie about medium brown, but now they all have the same color hair. It will probably change as they get older.

We had such a long safari just before Christmas, and we really went a lot of places. We were on our way to TAP retreat in Nairobi, but this time went around the lake on the west side, and on up into Uganda. We saw a Diamond Mine on the way up. The children loved it, but not because they were seeing diamonds. They had to go up and down many ladders amidst much dust, noise and dripping, and that is the part they liked! With that particular visit there were some "hard" parts. Just as we were leaving Dodoma where we had spent the night with some Language School friends, Dave saw that there was something in the engine that had to be welded together, so we didn't get off till noon. It was an all day trip, so along about 11 P.M. when we didn't know where we were on a lonely, swampy road Dave got too sleepy to go on, so we pulled off in a school driveway and spent the night. Five of us in our VW with our luggage! Once before we did that and I had forgotten how terrible it was! Dave and the children got some sleep, and I slept a bit too towards morning. Next morning Dave dug down into the bottom of a river bed to get some water for shaving so we got some pictures of that—we have learned not to travel without taking our own drinking water and food along too, so we fared alright. We did see some real diamonds that next day.

I think I did write you from Limuru, didn't I, so I probably told you about our Nile River trip and the crocodiles and hippos? Are you **sure** you can't come over yet before we go? We would just love to share some of these experiences with you. TAP retreat was so good—we'll miss it much when we get to the States. Don Jacobs is such a stimulating speaker and creative leader—we think very highly of him. Main idea from the retreat (did I tell you?) was the white man is very much needed here, but not very much wanted. Also, we probably have to bear some of the hostility engendered by the early colonialists and missionaries. The missionaries did so much good-personal sacrifices, massive evangelism, education, etc., but also some bad—treated the Africans as children, took tribal lands, tried to brand everything in the culture as "evil." I suppose it had to be a mixture of that type in order to accomplish so much in so short a time (much **was** accomplished), but now times call for a change in approach, much love, brotherhood, and understanding.

Love,
Flo

Last Wednesday , the nursing students had a little program, with a drum and some dancing. It was the first time we've seen it here and we thoroughly enjoyed it. Marie just got over chickenpox—think David's got it now because he's a bit lethargic today.

I think Hiram must be getting famous. We look forward to his concerts. We have somewhat mixed feelings about 111 Elfreth's Alley—we've had a taste of freedom now! Also worry a bit about schools for the children. How near are you to BSN? We are planning one more long safari to Mombasa in Kenya with Nevin Kraybill's in March.

You have never told me of some things you may want from here. Please hurry! Got a nice letter from Louise also one from Lois Kennell. Someone wrote that John Ruth's son may have a tumor. Is there any news of that?

(The Puzzle—we loved it—I couldn't get any work done for the day because it was there, tempting me! Finally got it together.)

Love, Flo

JORURNALING: SNAKES

1970

I was just covered with sweat and was so hot and scared. I had just killed the second of the little green snakes with the broom. I was just getting ready to put the children to bed, a little early, because Dave had to go to Kidugala to take a body back in the LandRover, because it wouldn't fit in Kleefeld's car, although Kleefeld had brought the man here, and he had died on the way here. Anyway, I was anticipating a nice long Sunday evening after the children were in bed. Just as we got over to David's bed, there went one of those despicable little green snakes in the manner I remembered so well from last year. I got all hot, screamed a little, the children had been playing nicely and screaming too, so I don't know if they screamed too. Anyway, I finally pinioned it down with the leg of one of the chairs and killed it, and turned around, and, there, closer to Anne's bed, wasn't there another one! I had sent Marie to get the broom, and with the handle of the broom killed that one. Then I made the children get up on the little round table in the middle of the room while I took out all the mats and rugs and looked around. I examined Anne's bed carefully, and then tucked her in with her mosquito net.

I had told David and Marie to try to keep Anne from being so scared, so they were saying things to her like, "Snake, no, no, eat you up," and, "If snake bite you then you get shot in the hospital and then you no die!" This was meant to be reassuring, but they were obviously trying to reassure themselves, and also obviously had heard a lot of talk about snakes!

Last year when we had those other four snakes, we made a fuss about the cracks near the ceiling, and insisted that a *fundi* (carpenter) come and seal up all those cracks. He did that, and we think he did a good job, so where in the world are these little green things coming from? That's what has me so terribly frustrated. If we only knew that, we could fight it. As it is, one is scared to reach anywhere today. As I am typing this, I keep watching and hoping, and not hoping, that another one will come, so I can see where it's coming from. I just hope I can persuade Dave now to take down all those beautiful flowers off the sides of the house. They couldn't possibly have come in the windows, because, unlike usual, I had the windows shut all day, and don't remember opening them even once.

While we were still in America, and while we were in language school in Nairobi, I used to think about snakes, but I would tell myself that really it's not so bad. Well, it has been much worse than anything I could have imagined. They are right in the house with you, and you just have this terrible feeling that you can't get away from them, and you walk around looking at the floor all the time.

Next time it was Bahtletti who found the snake. She was doing the usual cleaning, although it was on Thursday instead of Wednesday; because of the day she had off on Monday, we are a day behind schedule this week. It was about two and a half weeks ago that we saw the first one, and this is now the fifth one for this year. Last year we only saw four, and one of them was dead! I must say, I didn't get quite so panicky as I had—am I getting used to it? Probably, because I didn't discover and kill it myself. Anyway, as chance would have it, Mrs. L. happened to come over soon after. I thought she came to see it, because Rangnar, her son, had told her, I know, so I showed it to her. Later I found out she didn't really come for that, but to ask if Dave would like to eat with the German-Tanzanian-Meeting-People who were eating at their house, but after I see one of those snakes, I usually can't think of anything else for a while.

Anyway, as usual, she didn't see what I was making all the fuss about, and as usual this annoyed me considerably. I said that if she had snakes in her house she probably would feel as I did. This we discussed for a while, and then she left after we completed our "business." Afterwards, I said to Bahtletti, that Mrs. L., didn't think it was so serious.

That led to a most interesting discussion with Bahtletti. She said the Africans would probably consider this *uchawi*. She asked me if I knew this word, which I didn't but I looked it up in my Swahili dictionary. It means "sorcery, witchcraft, black arts, magic!" *Kumbe!* Then, she said that if an African has a big *shida* (trouble), he thinks it is this *uchawi*, and apparently this kind of recurring trouble is in this category! So then I asked her if Christians believe this too. She said *"wote"* (everyone). Then I asked her if she believed it, and she said *"Sijui"* (I don't know) but I got the distinct impression that she did. I asked her if the minister as well believed this and she said "yes". (I have never, to my knowledge, heard it mentioned in any connection from the pulpit, but you can't go by that since my Swahili leaves much to be desired.)

I asked her what people do if they do get *uchawi,* and asked her if they would go to an *Mganga* (doctor). She seemed very surprised that I even knew that word, and said, "Yes." (We had attended a series of lectures on African Culture by Don Jacobs while we were in language school, so I had at least heard of *Waganga* doctors.) Anyway, I asked her what he would do and she said he would, *"Mpe mtu dawa kwa kunywa*" ("give the man medicine to drink"). I asked her if he ever butchered an animal, and she was very surprised at this idea. I'm sure I read somewhere or heard somewhere that there are sacrificial animals involved in this *Waganga* business. But she said that the *Mganga* can give medicine so that cows can sleep outside and not be harmed by hyenas or other animals, and she knew of two or three men in **this** community who had done this, and whose animals sleep outside all the time, without harm. I am sure I don't know why they don't all just get some *dawa* (medicine) for their animals then, it certainly would be a lot easier to my way of thinking than to have to build a shelter for them; there must be more to this than meets the eye. I must ask her sometime if we ever get to talking about these things again. She also said that a person does not tell his family he is going to an *mganga*, he just goes. I don't know if they tell later or not. She also said, after I asked, that it costs a lot of money. Other things to go for are to have children, but only if you are married. I then asked her if you could go to get help in order to get a husband. She seemed surprised at that, so I said, "Do all women get husbands?" She sort of hedged on that one, and I'm not sure what she said, to tell you the truth, but she did say if a woman is not able to get a husband, she still tries to have a child. I suppose that is sort of self-explanatory about the husband bit. She herself has a child, now five years old, is not married, although the father of the child is, and was. She still plans to get married, I know, because she has told me so. I have heard that unmarried women who have a child already are usually taken as second wives. I personally hope that Bahtletti is not taken as a second wife–she seems like such a fine woman.

As for my own belief about the matter of the snakes, I think they're hatching out of eggs someplace, and coming in here instead of going out—poor things, one by one we're killing them. Wonder how many more there are. They are smaller around than a lead pencil, about the size of a number nine knitting needle, a little more than a foot in length, green as the leaves on a tree, light green underneath, and walk or crawl with their heads up. Wonder where they're coming in at! The kind of *dawa* I want is something to seal up every crack and pinhole in this house, and I'm going to fuss until I get it. I'm also going to keep asking Dave to cut down the bougainvillea and other flowers on the house, because I'm just sure they're the culprit. And, especially since if Bahtletti hadn't killed this last one, it would have gone under the door into his office.

Our conversation about things African continued in the kitchen. Bahtletti had brought us some *mboga* (vegetables) from her *shamba* (garden), because she knew we liked them. They are someplace between a squash and a pumpkin, and they make a delicious pumpkin pie. You can also eat them like squash with butter and salt, which I think is how the Africans eat them, sans the butter of course. While they are in the growing stage, the leaves, cooked together with some tomato, onion, milk or cream, and the blossoms (yellow), make a very delicious and tasty dish—at least to my way of thinking! It is much better than any spinach I ever tasted, cooked in any way. It is really surprising how many greens the Africans eat in their diet—they should really be getting enough iron. Every so often I ask Bahtletti to cook this for us, although actually I do most of the cooking myself. It never seems to turn out the same when I try to cook it. There is only one thing I improved upon (in my opinion anyway) and that is, I asked her to wash the leaves **before** she chopped them up. I just can't stand that gritty taste, and after that last *ndudu* (little bug) in it, I asked her to slightly modify her preparations! I suppose you could get some good protein out of those little bugs at that, if you didn't know it!

So I was cutting the "pumpkin" preparatory to cooking it for pie, and as I was taking out the seeds, I asked her if they ever eat the seeds. The other day she told me they usually take out the seeds (look like ordinary pumpkin seeds to me) and the stringy stuff inside. Well, she said in answer to my question, that the dried seeds are ground up and put in the meat of a woman who has just given birth in order to insure an adequate milk supply for the infant! Again, *kumbe*! Wonder what's in them? Maybe I'll have to dry some myself and send it to a drug company to be analyzed. She said you give only a little to those who seem to have an adequate milk supply, and a lot to those who don't seem to be getting enough. According to some medical "experts" in the States, African women bear, give birth to, and nurse their babies with **no** trouble whatsoever, and if we American women would only do as they do, we wouldn't have any trouble either! Since I have been here, I have certainly observed differently, but that's another chapter.

After this interesting bit of information I asked Bahtletti about other "native medicine" that I had heard so much about. Sometimes a patient will come into the hospital, very sick, and "native medicine" is blamed for the sickness, or at least lack of cure. This happens especially, I understand, with mothers having difficulty giving birth. Bahtletti said if there is difficulty giving birth, there is a *dawa* that can be given. She said the *wazee* (old people) know where to get it, and it is obtained from trees in the *pori* (wilderness, or places that are not farmed). She said the old people of her family know where to get it, and if they should die, she would buy it from the *wazee* of other families. She said they pass it on sometimes to younger members before they die. I suppose that would also bear investigation by some drug companies, if it has not already been done.

I saw another snake after that one—just out of the corner of my eye I saw it on the other side of the typewriter case—head up, just looking and waiting. I wonder what he was waiting for. What do they eat anyway? I made sure Dave saw that one, and he killed it himself with the broom. He never wants to believe me and always asks things like, "Was it really a snake?" and "Was it alive?" He toyed around a bit with it, with the broom, to see if it would attack, and we both saw that it certainly does attack, if attacked. Otherwise, I think there is some comfort in knowing that they will run and hide from people. Just the same, who wants to have a snake hiding in the corner of the room? For the moment at least, I am sewing and typing in another room—don't trust the area around my feet that I can't see. I have also placed all the *mikekas* (mats) and rugs outside on the porch. I want to see as much of the room in one sweeping glance as I can! If we only knew where they are coming in at. I haven't opened any windows for three days now. Glad we have at least little screens in to let in some fresh air. I also had Dave cut down the greens.

Missionaries are saying that they come in the front door! I suppose one day, three little green snakes decided to come in our house, followed each other in the door, went through the living room, or the bath and our bedroom, into the children's room! Ridiculous. But I suppose I shouldn't reject it so easily when I don't know myself where they did come in. But I'm just sure they didn't march in that door!

Whenever I go in that room, I look under all the beds and things. I can't reach into the children's closet with any comfort to get their clothes, but of course it must be done. As for the children themselves, they seem to have placed it in the back of their minds where they don't have to be bothered with the thought. The thought is less tolerable than the actuality. Perhaps they are simply not able to tolerate the thought of snakes in their room. After that first night, there has been no sleeping problem, and then it was only Marie and me that were troubled.

She woke up and kept saying she couldn't go back to sleep, and of course I couldn't either, so I asked her if she wanted me to come in and sit there. I sat there for a few minutes right beside her bed (close to where I killed the snake with the chair) and was mighty uncomfortable. I kept looking up at the ceiling to see if I could see anymore coming down, and then the mosquitoes kept pestering me. Every crack and curved line gave me a jolt!

We usually have a light burning in the night, ever since last year's snakes. Before that, sometimes, if it was a nice moonlit night we just opened the curtains and let the moonlight in, but after the other rash of four snakes, **I** wanted the light on. The children were doing fine accustoming themselves to the night without a light, but **I** wasn't. But then, they didn't have to get up in the night and walk around in their bare feet either!

Anyway, to continue with sitting up with Marie because she couldn't sleep, finally I asked her if she wanted me to get in her bed with her. She said yes of course, so I did. I was very much comforted! In fact, we laughed a little and started talking about snakes and other things, and she was talking a mile a minute. It was one of those times when we really felt close to each other. I told her that I had been having trouble sleeping too, and had moved close to Daddy. Then I said "Now don't you tell!" Of course, first thing in the morning she did tell Dave what I had said!

Finally, in order to make her stop talking, I turned my back, and we both relaxed a little. Then I said I was going to my own bed, and we both slept the rest of the night. That was after about 2:00 A.M., I think. I didn't sleep too easy, but at least I got a little sleep, although I kept waking up and looking out on that part of the floor of their room that I could see from my bed. Dave found another of the snakes in the bathroom yesterday, a week later. The children came running to tell me, because I'm sure he wouldn't have told me himself. They saw him trying to examine the fangs, but he finally said it's too small, and he can't tell if it's poisonous. As far as I'm concerned they are! But, maybe they are just a "harmless green house snake" as Don Jacobs told us they probably were, at TAP retreat last year.

We had been off visiting a local church, and came home afterwards, after having all doors and windows locked. That absolutely explodes the theory of them coming in the front door. (I never did believe it.) I haven't opened a window all week, and have conscientiously kept the door shut. Also, I check under every bed every morning these days, and behind doors, etc. So, I know it wasn't there this morning. If we only knew where they were coming from. I think they could provide us with a snake-proof house for the least! Nothing has bothered me here like this, and I am ready to pack up and go home, almost.

Mrs. L. came over right after Dave found the other one, and I told her it is almost more than I can take. She didn't say anything much, but did wonder if they could be coming up from below someplace. (She's the builder's wife.) Today we were talking about it again a little. Mrs. L. wondered why I am not getting used to these snakes. I must admit, it hurt me. Perhaps there is something wrong, and I should just take it in stride. Anyway, I asked Bahtletti if she could get used to snakes in the house and she said "*Sijui.*" ("I don't know.") (A typical response I might add.) Then I told her that someone had asked me why I wasn't getting used to the snakes, and she said, "*Pengine wanajua dawa.*" (Perhaps you want medicine.) I was just wondering what an African would say about getting used to snakes in the house, because I think they, too, are quite afraid of them, although perhaps not to the extent that I am, because they have grown up with them. They are much more afraid of cars, I suppose. At least, I have seen them run far off the road at the approach of a car!

I had just read Roseyeare's book, *Give Me This Mountain,* and she rejoices that she was able to suffer along with Christ (physically) and thus perhaps shoulder some of the guilt (as He did) of the early white exploiting settlers. Of course this book was written in retrospect, but in all fairness, she did go back again. Now, I wonder, this little thing of these snakes in the house, am I to suffer (actually) too? I don't think I can do it.

LETTERS

1970

Dave to Hiram

January 1970
Ilembula, Tanzania

Dear Hiram,

We are having heavy rains nearly every day and hot weather. It is good for the crops as the people are short of food from last year's poor crop. Several areas have near famine conditions.

Wednesday, I read *Time* and noted the bearishness of the market. Even IBM plummeted. I hope for the best. *Time* had a full page advertisement on UCC merger with Automation Center International, Zurich. I hope it is a good merger.

Two items I need from you if possible; first, is income and expenses for 1969 for the Federal Income Tax Form. Last week I received all the Federal tax forms in the mail. I think there is very little in the way of money, as there were no stock transactions. The second item is my U.S. Driver's License for 1969 and '70 for our trip home.

It is hard to believe there are only three more months to our stay here. The end is coming very fast. We must start packing and arranging things for the trip to the U.S.A. In spite of this, we are all continuing very busy with the patients and Hospital.

Greetings to the family.

Sincerely,
David

P.S. Florence had her sewing class just now so has typed this in a hurry as I want to get it in today's mail. A doctor and his doctor wife have arrived here from Holland and will be replacing us. I hope to turn things over to him as soon as possible so he has a chance to get in the groove before we leave.

March 2, 1970
Ilembula, Tanzania

Dear Hiram,

Thank you for your letter of February 17. Things are busy around here too, but of course not of the pace of the U.S.A.

The tax information has arrived together with the driver's licenses and medical license. I had also just received a U.S.

tax form from Washington for International residents. I was concerned about the licenses as there is so much red tape to get a new one if it lapses.

We are thankful that Nd and Edet are both alive. The Nigeria problem is certainly a black mark on African history. What is also disturbing is that many countries here have a similar potential problem, that of tribal conflict. Time will tell how these problems are solved. Kenya, Uganda, Ethiopia, and Sudan are examples. Tanzania has 130 tribes, some small and some large. But, fortunately, there are no two large tribes here; nor have the smaller tribes taken any sides in matters. Then there is also strong idealistic leadership in Dar es Salaam to attract allegiance.

Last weekend we took two days to beautiful mountains—70 miles from here. We visited a sheep-raising scheme on the plateau at 9,000 feet. There were many sheep (the children thought they looked like bears) and beautiful flowers, among them orchids. Then we went on to Mkete leprosarium for souvenirs and sightseeing.

In two weeks we leave for a two-week trip to Mombasa, along the Indian Ocean, to fish, swim, and hunt sea urchins, etc. We will go together with Nevin Kraybills of Shirati, and my two missionary Aunts also from Shirati.

As far as 111 Elfreth's Alley goes, we want to move in there the beginning of July. So the Lehmans may stay to the last week in June. Eventually though, we want to move to some open country, as this deep city is probably not the place for people like us. Just now we are working on our itinerary through Europe together with MTS.

Sincerely,
David

JOURNALING: NEW HOUSEGIRL

1970

Ilembula

*I*f I could only look on her as somebody to do the housework and let it go at that, it would certainly be a lot easier. But no, that first time she was late, I asked her "why" she was late. If I could only have said, "If you're late again you will be replaced," or "Half a day's salary will be taken off because you're late," or something like that. Then she had to tell me, after I asked, that her baby was sick. So then, I had to know details of course, and it turns out the baby is seven months old, and she has been leaving it in the care of another child, a five-year-old daughter. I told her that unless she gets someone to take care of the children she would not be able to work for us. I can't bear the thought of those little children alone there while she is here doing our work. Also, I gave her exact instructions of what to feed the baby (it had vomiting and diarrhea) and even fixed some weak orange juice, broth, tea, gave instructions how much to give, and when, etc. The child apparently recovered, but what bothers me is that if the mother hadn't been coming to work here, and had been breastfeeding the child, it probably wouldn't have gotten sick. Maybe.

This is the first month that she is working for us. I said I would give her a chance. Her story runs something like this: she is married with seven living children (two died). Her husband is in Mwanza, in Northern Tanzania, and there has married another wife. Although they have no children, he apparently prefers this second wife. Our housegirl was having trouble getting food and clothing for herself and the children so she followed him to Mwanza. I'm not sure how long she was there, but when she came home (so I was told by someone else) she said, all she got were beatings, another baby, and no clothes. So she came here to Ilembula again looking for work.

For a while she has been helping us part time by doing laundry, and I told her if she agreed to work for a while and learn from Bahtletti (who got married) how to do the work here, I would give her a trial in the house. Well, she was late again the other day, so I asked her why. She said she was writing letters and didn't know the time had passed! I'm sure she has no clock.

One of the things that bothers me is that every day we feed our dogs and cats meat and rice. The meat here is about 17 cents a pound in American money, and seems quite cheap to use. In fact, one time when we were on holiday, one of the other missionaries had a "fit" that we weren't feeding our animals more meat and milk. I was very angry with her and mentioned something about starving children around and she said, all right then, give your money for them, and flounced out the door.

I am just sure that we feed our animals more meat than the housegirl gives her children. The other day I couldn't stand it any longer, so I gave her a chunk of our meat. She told me one day when I asked, that the meat is too expensive and that's why they don't eat more. And I can't lose weight!

JOURNALING: MAMA R.

and other rambling thoughts
about Ilembula, Tanzania

1970

I don't know if I could be that calm if my child, my first son, had just died the day before. She was just squatting there, that young woman, *kanga* over her head, but her face seemed different, maybe from crying, and I didn't recognize her at first. Coming in from the bright sun, into the darkened house that had the curtains over the window, the three black women looked very much alike. I said, "I'm looking for Mama R.----," and then someone said, "*Huyu ni Mama ----*" ("This is Mama R.----"). Then I looked closely, and then I saw that it was the face I knew so well.

My housegirl, T.----, had asked me yesterday if I had heard the news about the girl whose picture I had painted. It took me a minute to register whom she meant, but then I realized that she meant this particular young mother whom I had known, Mama R.----, and I said what news? She said that the day before, when I had asked her to take some tumblers to one of the other missionaries, she had seen Mama R.---- carrying her child. Of course, to see a woman carrying her child was not unusual because the women here usually carry their children on their backs. They carry them in a manner that is very easy and secure for the child, by tying them on with a piece of cloth. It is also secure for the mother, and leaves her hands free to work, or carry things on her head, or do whichever of the many hard physical activities that women in this country must do. At one time I felt sorry for the women who worked so hard, and said to Dave what a hard lot in life they

Bahtlet carrying Anne Harnish, Tanzanian style.

had because they had to work so hard. In my opinion their life is hard because the tasks they do are so far beyond my own stamina, although perhaps I might be able to do work this hard if the survival of my children and myself depended upon it. At least my own mother was able to chop wood, feed the chickens, milk the cows, light the fire, hoe the garden, can 300 quarts of peaches, rock the baby, teach a Sunday School class, sometimes help with the harvesting, rear eight children, clean the house, sew the clothes, pump the water, and help the neighbors, among other tasks.

But Dave said that it's not the hard work that makes the people die young here, but the malnutrition and ignorance about causes of disease. After some discussion and more discussion about it, I realized that this is true. Then I began to pity **myself** for not having the strength to do what they are doing! Now I look at their strong lean bodies, and envy them their strength.

Concerning children that are carried on the backs of the mother, I have seen hundreds, and of those, there are only three that I can recall at the moment who were crying. One was far away and I don't know why the child was crying, but I do know the mother had a debbie of water which she was carrying up the hill and maybe she couldn't attend to the needs of the child just then, and he was screaming loudly.

Tanzanian women carrying heavy pot, plus her child.

The other two were afraid of me—my white face I guess. (Although really, I consider my face sort of pinkish, and not really white.) While I am talking about secure babies, I have seen only two thumb-sucking African babies, and one of these was an orphan in the hospital. Their babies that are *bebad* (carried) on the back can suck milk from the mother's breast anytime they want to, and therefore the sucking in a way is as much for the pacifier-effect than for actual nourishment. It has actually enhanced my faith in a pacifier as we Americans use it, because somehow in our culture, to have an infant constantly sucking at the breast is now taboo—even if it is for nourishment as God obviously intended it. It is probably **more** taboo among our Mennonite group than among some other more "liberal" groups, both in and out of the religious community. Why should this be? I have thought about it a lot since I first came here three years ago.

But T.---- continued with what she had said about seeing Mama R.---- carrying the child. What she hadn't known, and what the news was really about, was that the child she was carrying home on her back, had just died, and she was carrying him home to be buried! I have seldom heard anything so sad as that mother carrying her dead child. I was so sad myself. All last night I kept thinking about Mama R.---- and Fexus, which was the name of the little boy. This morning I asked T.---- if it was really true. Although my conversational Swahili is passable, still there are times when I hear what hasn't been said. But T.---- said, "do you think I am telling lies?" I told her that I just wished that it wasn't true, because she seemed a little offended that I had asked her if it was really true.

The first time I recall seeing Mama R.---- was after we had been here about six months or so, when I first started having my sewing class over at the church. I remember her well because she was so young and pretty, and had such a nice baby. At that time the baby was only five months old, but he was already sitting very well by himself, and we discussed the fact that he was developing skills early as compared to American standards. I also remember her because she was the first one of the mothers to cut and sew a dress for herself, rather than just for her child. It was a purple dress, cut from Jinja cloth which the women had provided themselves, and it was made on a shift pattern, sent by my friend, Janie, from the U.S. I don't think she did a terribly good job of sewing it, but I never really saw it right after it was finished, although I asked her to bring it. Later when I did see it, it had been washed and washed, and apparently worn many times. I was pleased by that because it meant she had made something very useful.

It was also at that first meeting, or one of the first meetings, that in my ignorance I asked her if she had had a picture taken yet of the child. I was probably trying out my new Swahili. At that time none of the words had yet taken on their true meanings, but seemed like syllables only; the meaning attachment came later, gradually. I thought the child so cute, that I simply stated my own first reaction to cute children, "Let's get a picture." I know now that would have been completely out of the question for her, both in terms of expense and opportunity. Her reaction to my question was very interesting. She said she would "*Ngoja mpaka nitaona kama atakae*" (Wait until she saw if he would remain). Did she mean she'd wait until she saw if he'd live? I wonder if she ever did take a picture of him.

After that, I used to see her from time to time. I remember once she came for some thread or something, and just sort of stood around. She didn't have Fexus with her that time, and said he was sick. When I asked her what was the matter with him she said vomiting and diarrhea. So then we talked a bit, and I gave her some instructions about withholding food until the vomiting stopped and then to give tea and lemon juice. I went and got a lemon from one of the neighboring missionary's trees and gave it to her. Later, when I saw her after a few days time, she was very grateful and said that the child had completely recovered. If only these young mothers could get some help in treating these simple diarrheas. Of course, prevention is the answer to many of the diarrheas, but not all.

We in the U.S., have diarrheas and vomiting too, and we supposedly know how to prevent these things, or do we? But even if one did know, in a set-up such as theirs, how could they be prevented. A mud hut, with a hard-packed earth floor, no place to put your baby to play except in the dirt, and the only water in the house is that which was carried on your head from the nearest river. How could you wash your baby, and your hands in order to prevent these diseases? I have always said, if I were in charge of this country, the first thing I would do would be to establish some sort of water system to every home. My finite mind cannot understand why each of these houses can't have a pump in front of their house, or maybe one for every five houses or so, such as our own ancestors in America had. There is some very valid reason for this I am sure, or I would like to be sure, otherwise why hasn't it been done? (No doubt economic, as are all other stated reasons for not getting things done.)

They have started a system down at the river now for the "village." We always are afraid our children will fall in the deep hole when we take our walks to the river now. However, from the missionaries here, I have heard little but criticism about this project and why don't they do it this way and why don't they do it that way, and it won't work, and the village people will just throw rocks into it. And I'm just as bad, because I criticize the missionaries for criticizing! But, I do rejoice to think that perhaps the villagers will be getting a more adequate and good supply of water. As a matter of fact, when they carry their water from the river, that is the same river that they wash their clothes in, that the cows drink from, and it's dirty, and they take their baths in, as well as some people using it for a *choo* (toilet), I am sure.

When I think of my own childhood though, we certainly played in creeks and streams that were nothing but mud. Also the pigs and cows used this same stream and we loved it. But now I can't stand anything but crystal clear water! Also, we didn't use that water for drinking and cooking, but certainly we got plenty of it in our mouths when we were playing there. But, there was no *bilharzia*, and very few snakes, although there were definitely some. I can remember only one poisonous snake from my childhood, although there were some harmless garden snakes that we were also frightened of. Here I'm really panicky about the snakes, but our children don't seem to be. In fact, telling them to stay out of the deep grass seems to go in one ear and out of the other.

Mama R---- came to our sewing class more or less regularly. I always appreciated her because I could understand her Swahili. I don't know if it was better than that of the others or whether she could just talk to *Wazungu* (Europeans) better. She did work for some missionaries some years ago, although to this day I doubt whether she can be more than about 20 or 21 years old. At the sewing times, if an issue came up I always more or less waited to see what she had to say. They usually spoke Kibena (a tribal language) amongst themselves. Once in a while, if I knew what the topic of conversation was about, I could get some inkling of what was being said by their expression, although more often, I couldn't. If I asked they would usually tell me. But once, and the only time, Mama R---- apologized to me for their speaking Kibena, because she said they could say things so much better. When she voiced her opinion about the matters that were being discussed, usually it was what I wanted to do anyway. Maybe she was just sensitive to what I wanted, I don't know. Anyway, I considered her an intelligent and sensitive person who often acted as a self-appointed spokeswoman for the group. I am quite sure the women themselves did not feel that way about her. I must say, at times she seemed almost, what I would call, sullen.

Once she was in a play the women of the church gave, and she seemed so young, slender and vivacious, that even my husband asked about her. She played the part of one of the women of the Bible who has an evil spirit, but after seeing Jesus, is cured. She was so joyous after being cured—laughing, dancing, singing, in the church. Another time when I was to read something as part of another of their plays, it was she who nodded at me when the time came to tell me it was now my turn. And once, when I sang with them and forgot my book, she offered me hers, when the others simply ignored me or maybe were afraid to offer me theirs. I appreciated this, because I truly wanted to be accepted by their group. However, I didn't think it would have been possible to be truly a part of the group—such is the order of things between missionaries and the local people. I did feel very proud that they permitted me to sing with them and enjoyed learning their songs from rote—their harmony (4-part) was excellent, although there were some very grating voices. When they were first learning a song their voices would be soft, lovely and hesitant. Later when they knew the songs, well, it didn't always sound as nice.

Another contact I had with Mama R. was somewhat indirect. Our housegirl, at that time, was getting married, and we needed to find someone else, and this can be a pressing problem. The news was apparently out in the African community long before I knew anything about it, because people began to ask me for work. The president of the women's organization of the church also asked me to give her daughter work who had just come back from attending school at Kidugala. This I did not want to do, although I did not tell her so directly, but only said that I wanted to think about it. The thought of our present housegirl, T---- had already entered my mind, because she was helping do the laundry on

Mondays; and, in fact, we did hire her eventually—whether this was a wise choice is hard to say at this point.

Having worked with this president of the women's association, it became evident quickly that she was eager to get clothes for her own family, with not an awful lot of regard for those who were more needy. Why, I don't know, I felt that this business of sharing with the needy is one place where expatriate Christians do have a role to play. One wonders sometimes if they do have a role. Yet, how can this be taught with all of our affluence? But I mentioned again and again and again that the clothes were meant for the people who needed them, and not for the people with money, for there are people here with money, relatively speaking. She herself has a steady job at the local Lutheran school, and her son is one of the tribal dressers with a steady income. Her daughter-in-law had taken several lengths of cloth when they were supposed to take only one, and had not paid for them, even the small token fee that had been agreed upon. This year however, the president said that the daughter had paid for all of them and she did give me money.

Others also took cloth without sewing anything and without paying—I must say I was a bit hurt, also a bit educated to the fact that I must be a bit more careful how this cloth that was given with such Christian love from friends and relatives in the States was distributed. If those people who took the cloth needed it badly, I am only too happy if they got it. It never was intended that any payment be made. However, if they stole it, this will always be on their consciences. Better to have said, "I need this, but can't pay for it."

So it was, that when this president asked to have her daughter work here, it didn't seem desirable to me to give favors. However, the repercussions were rather large. It seems that she thought that Mama R---- had asked to work here, and had been granted employment by me. Now as it happens, we had considered employing Mama R---, even Dave suggested her. However on one occasion she had agreed to work here when our former housegirl wanted to take a short safari someplace, but on the morning of the day she was to work, she sent a message saying that she was not able to work. I had also heard that she had been sick a lot at the time of her former employment, so all things put together I did not want to hire her as our housegirl, although I was really very fond of her as a person. Also, she had not asked for employment.

This president of the women's association then sent her son, the tribal dresser (to whom she always refers as *mgonga* (doctor)), to talk to me and to tell me what an awful person Mama R---- was. I assume she sent him, how else would he have known anything about it, and also what other interest could he have had than that his sister get a job here? We have learned that the jobs with the missionaries are very much to be desired.

This son, spoke on and on and on. At first I was happy to see him. He is located at a clinic that the children and I have visited several times with Dave and he has always given us fruit and things like that, because it is a good fruit-growing area. I had no reason but to welcome him. But when he began to ask me whether Mama R---- had asked for work here, and to say that why should she be asking for work when her brother is supporting her, and that she tells lies, lies. And with this last statement in order to ensure that I had truly understood through my dim Swahili he pointed to his tongue and showed how it was twisted!

It was at that point that I was wishing him godspeed, and hurry up, and trying still to be polite, although I was really getting angry and wished that I had after all hired the girl (Mama R----), I told him that it was the business of my husband and myself whom we hired, and not his. I also told him that she had not asked for work here, but he chose not to believe that.

A day or two after that, maybe it was the next day, the missionary pastor here, along with an elder from the church and the pastor from the church came to me and asked me if the girl has gotten employment here! It really angered me that the family of the president of the women's organization had carried this thing this far. It seems they were having some kind of a *shouri* (investigation) at the church in which many things were being discussed about her. The child, Fexus, was her illegitimate child, which I had known almost from the first, but she had never admitted who the father of the child was. Apparently now, with this kind of interrogation going on, she finally admitted who the child's father was. A real witch hunt!

My housegirl at that time said, when I asked her why she was being interrogated, that it was because the father could then be forced to support the child. I was upset about the whole affair and feeling very sorry for Mama R----, because it seemed that everyone was pointing a condemnatory finger at her. This includes our housegirl, although at other times they had seemed like very good friends. That particular housegirl also had an illegitimate child, at that time about five years old, but everyone knew who the father was—apparently he had been a former cook with a missionary. Fexus at that time must have been about a year and a half old. When these "learned" men came to me, I told them that she had not asked for work here, but I felt like saying what business is it of yours. I did say that I had already told the son this, and they seemed very surprised; apparently he hadn't told them that I had said that.

I was ready to go right over to the church and defend this poor girl. But nobody asked me to go, and probably it's a good thing because by that time I **was** upset. What did it have to do with anybody if she wanted to get a job! It seems to me they should have been glad that she was that ambitious. To me it seems that jealousy played a large part of this whole affair. I too am subject to much jealousy all the time. Is this what it does to people? Probably there was much more to this affair than I knew about, but this is the way it seemed to me. One of the other missionaries said she was afraid I had gotten involved, and I said I was very sorry that I wasn't involved. How can you accomplish anything if you don't get involved in a few affairs, and suffer a little personal unpleasantness once in a while for what you know is right?

I heard no more about that particular affair from anyone except from Mama R---- herself. A day or two later, she came, and **did** ask for work! By that time we had already made up our minds that we would hire T----. I don't know if Mama R---- was just playing it cool all that time and had planned to ask for work or not. I asked her what the big *shouri* was all about, and she said she guessed it was because they wanted me to hire Annetta, the daughter of the women's president. This is exactly what I had also surmised, but I shall never know if it was the truth. Mama R----'s response did reinforce my suppositions about the *shouri*. At our next sewing meeting, both the president and Mama R---- were there, and things seemed about as normal, although I thought Mama R---- seemed a bit subdued. The president, as an "elder," had been at the actual inquisition.

About that same time I had begun to give some of the women napkins and things to sew, for which I paid them, and then resold them. We also did some necklaces out of seeds, and I was trying to think of other ways for these common ordinary working mothers, some of whom could not speak Swahili, and none of whom could speak English, to earn some money. Some of them cannot even write their own names, and I think this is one of the sadnesses of this earth. In order to give Mama R---- more money, and because I had wanted to paint someone's picture for a long time, I asked her if she would pose for me to paint her picture. It was a new experience, because I had never painted a picture from a real person before, although I do like to dabble with paints. It is also a bit embarrassing to stare at someone's face so pointedly! (Once in the States I went to a beginning painting class and I was chosen to be painted. All I could do was sit up front and smile self-consciously.) The picture turned out fairly well, although it doesn't look too much like **her**. She seemed pleased to do it, and was surprised at the finished picture. It seems all the more surprising that I didn't recognize her at first in her house the other day after her son died.

The next thing I heard about her was that perhaps she would be getting married. I mentioned before that she was very pretty, and also could be quite lively and carry on an interesting conversation when she wanted to. She must have been lonely at times, for who isn't. I had heard that her father had either died or ran away when she was only a small child. About the possibility of marriage, I heard later that the man to whom she would be married would not consent unless she would leave Fexus. She was not willing to do that—actually he hadn't even been weaned at that time, although he was well over a year.

At the time that I gave the sewing materials to the women of the church to carry on for themselves (because we were leaving for America) there were some women who had not paid the fee that the group had agreed upon. When I gave the record books to the president (this occurred about a month or so ago), she was very careful to ask if Mama R--- had paid her debt. **Many** others had not, and why then did she ask specifically about her? Fortunately, Mama R---- had paid hers. When I asked her why, she said that Mama R--- had run away, leaving Fexus at home. Later when I asked T---- about this, she said that she had heard that Mama R---'s brother had been beating her, and maybe this is why she left.

JOURNALING: DIGGING

1970

Ilembula

*T*his is the third week now for the digging at the hospital. The first week everyone was taken by surprise. Mama L. came "storming" over to me to complain about Dave. You see, it was his idea. At first, it was discussed in a committee meeting which was held here one night. To that committee meeting, no one really wanted to come because they were not informed until the last minute. But most did come, *i.e.*, the missionaries, and they discussed various and sundry things. Among the things that were discussed was the plan of the new maternity building under construction and the placement of toilets, utility rooms, etc., for the most convenience. Well, Dave introduced the idea of the hospital staff doing a little digging themselves, going along with the idea of Nyerre's self-help "Ujamaa." The idea was tossed around a bit. L. (the matron) said the nursing students must help, and G. (directress of Nursing School) mustn't keep the students like "little queens," and the matter was dropped. Dave apparently took this

Digging at Ilembula Hospital for new wing.

as the go-ahead signal, and a week or so later everybody's name appeared on a list outside the matron's office saying that they were expected to dig on a certain date.

The first I knew anything about it was when L. came home for lunch the day before the event was to occur and said to me, "Dave has put your name on the list for digging. Is that all right with you?" Well, as usual I didn't know anything about it either, wasn't consulted beforehand, and must admit it made me angry. Then, from someone, I heard there was to be tea served. Later, when Dave came home, I asked him about it. By that time I had cooled off a bit. I asked him who was to serve the tea, and he mumbled something about "I'll have to ask L." and I knew immediately that more trouble was in the offing. When L. came over after a while about something else, to borrow butter I think, I asked her who was going to serve the tea. She, in a very haughty way, said, "Your husband said there was going to be tea, and now he'll have to see where he gets it!" It made me so aggravated at her, and I did an about face in my thinking, and decided then and there that **I** was going to serve the tea. Especially since I can't do much digging (I did do a little!), I was eager, actually, to serve the tea.

Well, that first week, quite a few people showed up to dig, including **this** family: father, mother, and three children. Dave shoveled like a trooper, and the children had the time of their lives playing in all that dirt. I shoveled around a little, but when I saw all the hospital staff there, I decided I had better go home and make tea! So, I went home to do it. Originally I had planned to make a little fire right there, and heat a big *sufarini* of tea on it, but Bahtletti wasn't there, and I am anything but a fire-lighting "fundi". Besides, I couldn't carry that big *sufarini* of tea up that big hill. So I ended up lighting the fire in the stove here, and making the tea here, transporting it up the hill to the hospital where they were digging, by putting it into empty milk tins. Lo, and behold, when I got there about 5:00, everybody was so hot they wanted ice water or juice! Dave wanted to know why didn't

I bring cold tea! Anyway! After all the fuss they should have been glad I was bringing any kind of tea!

After all, I had enough trouble making it. The Africans usually boil their milk, sugar and tea all together and drink it that way. So I tried it too, and probably was successful. However, at one point, someone knocked at the door before I got one of the big *sufarinis* to boil; while I was answering the door the pot began to boil, and with all that milk and sugar in it, it boiled out all over the stove and all over the floor. What a mess! Bahtletti cleaned it up afterwards. Incidentally the man at the door was bringing us some papayas; he was the dresser from the dispensary at Brandt. We do love papayas, so I can't complain.

Soon after the milk stuff boiled over, Bahtletti arrived. I was sorry I hadn't asked her to return sooner, but after all, she needs some time off too. She helped me make more tea and carry it up. She carried three tins at a time on a tray on top of her head, of course. Well, so many people wanted water, that we got water for the first crew. Unboiled water! I said to Bahtletti, "Shall we use unboiled water?" And she said, "*Wote hutumia nyumbani.*" ("All drink it like this at home.") And then there was the matter of the cups. Well, the notice had said everyone was to bring their own cup. Just in case, I took a few extra cups for those who may have forgotten theirs. **One** person, out of 25, brought a cup. They used the cups I brought over and over! I said to Bahtletti, "How shall we wash them?" So she took a little of the (unboiled) water and poured it in the cup, and dumped it out. Presto, washed! It did look pretty grimy with all those tea leaves in it when you were getting a cup of tea. I tried not to think of all those diseases that are transmissable by mouth, and I sure kept our children from drinking from these much-used cups. I was hard pressed to keep Anne from doing it however; as a matter of fact, this third time (when I wasn't present) Dave found her playing at the place where he said the sewage from the hospital (!) spilled over, and later eating a *mendozi* (donut), with those same unwashed hands.

Bahtletti said later that some people said the tea was too sweet, while others said there wasn't enough sugar in it! They were entitled to one cup of tea, but some drank as many as five, according to Bahtletti. One young man asked if there wasn't some bread too! Bahtletti said emphatically, "*Hamna!*" ("We don't have any!")

On the whole, the digging that first time was a success. We thought we had dug quite a big hole! Two *wazungu* (white people) besides ourselves showed up—L. and H. (Swedish missionaries). As for L., she carried dirt and carried dirt and carried dirt until she was red in the face. She was trying to prove something, but I suppose we all were. As for H., she was the **one** missionary who didn't grumble about it, but simply marched up there with her *jembe* (hoe), in a working dress with all her hair tied up, and got to work. She even drank tea along with the best of them! Bravo.

The second time, I understand, L. herself made the tea, or juice, or water, or whatever. I really didn't hear too much about it. Now, this third time, Mama L. made the tea **and** *mendozis*! She, who was so ired up that her name even appeared on the list at all! You recall, I mentioned that she came to see me about it, very angry, after the first list went up with her name on it. It so happened that Dave went to an outlying clinic the day the list went up, and she told me that she had tried to catch him before he went but missed him. Lucky Dave! She can really let loose if she wants to, although I don't know if she would have, at a *mzungu* (white person). Anyway, she had calmed down a bit by the time she came to see me, but was still mad. I tried to calm her ruffled feathers, told her that she was right to be angry not to have been consulted (she said she would have been glad to make tea if she had been asked nicely, and that I was trying to salvage the situation as best I could. She said G. was burned up about the whole situation.) Actually, I did feel badly about the situation.

Anyway, things went as scheduled that time, and lo and behold, this third time I find that she is making the tea and *mendozis* herself! To top it all off, on the day that the third digging should have taken place, but didn't, G. had all her nursing students out there digging! Guess she didn't want to be left out after all! Dave hadn't even noticed it (we happened to be on safari to Mbeya that day). So, she came to him, and told him, and asked if he hadn't noticed the big hole they dug. He hadn't, but being diplomatic (sometimes) he said he had. Oh well, the hole is getting dug, isn't it? And the maternity wing will get built, won't it? If the money comes in. But that's another chapter.

JOUNRALING:
WHY I CHOSE TO TEACH
MY CHILD MYSELF

1970

Ilembula

*E*ver since we have arrived at Ilembula at this "isolated" spot in Tanzania, the problem has existed for us: what type of schooling should our daughter receive. I was very verbal in discussing this problem with other *wazungu* parents, since it concerned me deeply. I particularly attempted to discuss it with those who were confronted with the same problem, or who had already sent their children to a school, referring specifically to missionary families. I was deeply intrigued by statements that a person might make, who himself had been sent to boarding school.

On the whole, those people with whom I spoke were somewhat surprised that this question should be troubling me. Most of them spoke well of the boarding school situation, usually with the idea that there was little or no choice, so it simply had to be accepted, viz, to send a child to boarding school was the best to be done under the circumstances. With the exception of a German family from here, whose children are now in universities or have graduated from them, we are the only parents with whom we are acquainted who chose **not** to send their child to a boarding school. We should like to suggest that there has been an alternative for us.

The local school is taught in Swahili. While there might have been certain advantages in sending her to this school—such as friendships, more involvement and deeper understanding of the local culture—it still did not seem to truly prepare her for the role she will probably ultimately play, *i.e.,* living in an English-speaking culture. Perhaps one should say "possibly" instead of "probably." From this vantagepoint, it seems quite possible that she will live in a non-English speaking community.

To have sent her to boarding school was a choice that was real, because MCC would have paid the fees; instead, they have paid the price of the Calvert Correspondence Course, since we opted for this. The nearest school for American children that we would have been able to send her to is about 500 miles away—two to three days away by car. The Mennonite School, where most of our (Mennonite) friends in this country send their children, is at Nairobi, 800 miles away—three days' journey by car. The children whom we have seen who are attending there seem happy, at least on the surface. The house-parents are well chosen and qualified; we know some of the teachers personally, and one was even one of my husband's teachers when he was a school child himself in Pennsylvania. We felt that this particular boarding school was excellent.

Why then, did we not send our child there? I must admit, that possibly in great measure the reasons for keeping our child at home may be grossly selfish. My heart simply froze at the thought of sending the child to a place, no matter how "good," where for months on end there would be no possibility of seeing her or communicating directly with her, no possibility of watching her growth, her social development, or helping her face her burdens. And, no matter how perfect the house-parents were said to be, I could not help thinking that they were **substitute** parents. Also, what about the fact that this particular child was sent by God to this particular (imperfect) family? If God has caused these particular chromosomes to form this child in this family, does then not that family have the responsibility for the education and upbringing of the child insofar as it is able? Let me hasten to add that not all parents want the responsibility of educating their children, nor, with their particular qualification should they; perhaps this too should be said about our family. Nevertheless, we decided that it was better that the child stay here, at the age of six years. Had she been older, perhaps another decision would have been made.

May I please state some advantages that I feel have been accrued by virtue of the fact that she has been taught at home? She has lived and moved in a culture composed mostly of black people, and also some from other European countries, which is different from her own. How has this benefitted? An example: This morning, she (Marie) and some friends cooked rice over an outdoor fire which they lighted themselves, using the local earthern cooking pot—round bottom—over three stones. They (I shall include our 5-year-old son (David) and other daughter (Anne) who is three, and use "they") have spent many hours digging clay from the ground, grinding it, and forming little pots and figurines from it. After drying the objects for a period of several days, they "fire" them in our fireplace, or woodburning kitchen stove. Some of these things have broken during the firing process because the pieces were not properly dried, this being a great educational process.

They have learned to speak Swahili, the national language, so that now they can converse quite competently at their own developmental levels. Because they have played with Swedish children, they have also learned quite a lot of the Swedish language, although we are really in a poor position to judge just how competent their knowledge is. They themselves contend that they can understand "everything!"

It is a pity that they will probably forget these languages as quickly as they learned them when we return to the States. However, they will have some concept of the fact that there **are** other languages, and just because one cannot understand another person does not mean that he is someone to be distrusted. Compare this facility with the language, which was picked up in ordinary play, with taking an hour or so of Swahili per week in a school.

They have worshiped with the African children in Sunday school. This then is where some of those "poor children" live for whom money has been given in the States. Here too, the children give pennies; and sometimes an ear of corn or an egg. They have learned many Swahili songs and some Swedish. These we have taped in an attempt to keep alive at least that aspect of their being here.

They have learned to like mangoes, guavas, and papayas picked right from the tree as the local people do. They have seen cassava planted and harvested and have learned to like it ground up and cooked as ugali. They have seen corn planted, cultivated by hand (hoe), and have learned to like the corn ears very much which have been

Flo and Dave Harnish, standing with children Marie, Anne, and David by papaya tree.

charred a bit by an open fire. They have seen coconuts harvested from very tall trees, and they have seen dugout canoes being fashioned.

They have seen shepherd boys watching their sheep and cows and goats, some with bows and arrows. They have seen people walking great distances on foot paths much as in the time of Jesus, and have understood why it may be necessary to "wash the dust from one's feet" after a journey. They have seen blind people being led by other people, and they have seen people who have literally had not enough clothes

Women preparing food for cooking ugali, *from cassava root. Cassava grows under dry conditions.*

Anne Harnish, looking to see what's going on with woman and baby grinding cassava for ugali.

to wear. They have been able to share some of their own clothing. They have seen mud houses built, and have visited in a few mud thatched roof homes. They have seen medical needs—who knows, perhaps they too, like their father, will respond to this need when they have the ability.

They have taken long safaris with the family group since schooling was flexible; perhaps our daughter might not have been able to take these trips had she been in boarding school. On these trips they have seen many things. The so-called "zoo" animals have been observed in their native habitat. A boat ride on the Nile River amidst crocodiles and hippopotamuses proved educational for all the family. One child has fed an elephant (not a caged one), they have stayed in a hut where the elephants ate acacia buds from the roof,

On safari—Anne, David, Marie, Dave Harnish. Inspiring scenery.

and they have seen an elephant charging and heard him trumpeting.

They have crossed flooded rivers in a car, have crossed wide ferries, and have been stranded in the wilderness overnight in their car. They have traveled on bumpy, dusty, roads where overturned trucks and buses are a common sight. They have taken a 22-hour non-stop bus ride jammed in with people of many nationalities. They have seen diamonds being mined, and have taken LandRover rides in terrain that would not be accessible to other cars, and they have seen some of the most beautiful scenery in the world.

Spontaneously they have become collectors. They are collecting rocks, seeds, stamps, insects, napkins, bird nests, and sea shells. They are avid bird watchers—an activity that has evolved as a family activity. There have been times when we could scarcely get our meals eaten because of the distraction

of watching the Weaver birds in the thorn tree right outside our dining room window. Excitement is great when someone discovers a new bird. Once, unbelievably, a very beautiful bird flew into the room through the open window, was uninjured, and shortly thereafter escaped from the hands of our son through an open door. They

Harnish children feeding geese at Ilembula.

Marie, Anne and David Harnish, holding household chickens and cat at Ilembula.

David Harnish holding family's rooster in Ilembula.

Flo, Anne, Marie, David and Dave Harnish. The family in front of a pointsettia plant in Ilembula.

have pets—dogs, cats (with kittens), ducks, turkeys, rabbits, and have seen the python sleeping in the cage of the rabbit after he had swallowed one of the rabbits and was too "fat" to escape! They have seen huge poinsettias in full bloom, and beautiful purple jackarani trees, whose blooms last for months.

They have seen airplanes and helicopters land and take off on what passes as an airstrip, and have seen doctors and patients come and go. They have seen the doctors who've emerged join their own father in work at the hospital and have eaten with these doctors, nurses, and pilots. They have seen their father work in the hospital and have worked with him caring for animals and garden, as well as seeing him frequently during the day (incidentally, a situation unlike that in America).

Academically speaking, there has been little pressure. It remains a constant paradox to me to hear people saying that the child in the home situation does not have the stimulation and pressures to learn as the child in school does, while at the same time leading educators like John Holt make statements of this type: "In some [better] schools children are freed from the kind of relentless and unending competition with other children that turns most classrooms into unbelievable nightmares." (*Family Circle*,

"Is School Doing Your Child More Harm Than Good?" September, 1969, p. 34)

We have attempted to provide an academic atmosphere in which the child has been free to explore his surroundings, free to ask questions, free to learn at her own pace. This has been done in part by the fact that school is held only for a few hours in the morning, leaving the rest of the day for activities. Recently we have instituted a reading-rest period for an hour after lunch as well, for the entire family. At times I have wondered what other children, who are in school for an entire day, are learning that our child is not. I hope, however, that our child is getting the personal attention which is so highly recommended and always striven for in the usual classroom, but never quite achieved. I might add at this point that the Correspondence Course which we have used has amply supplied us with materials unavailable here, viz., good scissors, paper, construction paper, rulers, newsprint, crayons, paints, etc., as well as textbooks, workbooks. The Teacher's Manual is very explicit, and is geared to the non-teacher mother.

There have been some misgivings in this venture of home teaching. Will our child be able to fit into a regimented classroom situation after having had much freedom? Perhaps, if she is on an academic par, she will survive. Has so much time been spent with me that the close association creates a dependency? Has there been enough association with peer groups? Perhaps association with African and Swedish children has been enough compensation. Also, what right does a mother have to give her full attention to one child to the exclusion of the others? This particular problem was more acute in the beginning when the youngest child was one year old and the other three years old. At this point, the second child is also in school (kindergarten) and the youngest is able to color, paste, etc. There have been occasions when guests arrived, thus necessitating extra cooking and entertaining which have interrupted the daily schedule. I have needed to make it understood, that, although we are in our own home, we are nevertheless having "school."

May I add a postscript that differs somewhat from the matters that I have mentioned above. Concerning "foreign missionaries," I feel that the day of sacrifice is probably past, except for two factors; the separation from one's "tribe" family and friends is difficult; in the matter of educating one's children, if this entails sending them to boarding school, there is true sacrifice. But who can say that living in an environment such as this, where your house is the finest in the village, and when you have servants to help with household and garden tasks is sacrifice? Distinct advantages are guaranteed MCC income, travel, and language study.

Once, a missionary mother (whose name I have fortunately forgotten) told me that the one thing she can never forgive herself for is having sent her young child to boarding school.

LETTERS

1970

April 7, 1970
Ilembula, Tanzania

Dear Janie,

I can't remember quite when I last heard from you, but it does seem like a long time. The same goes for any letters I have written to you lately, I am sure. We just got back last Friday night from our last holiday here which was to Mombasa, Kenya. I suppose one could say it is the "Atlantic City" of East Africa, however, there are no crowds or anything like that. In fact, it is a beautiful, unspoiled beach. It was really an education for us, because as far as I am concerned at least, the only times I have been to the ocean have been the two times Dave and I went with you. You will probably find that hard to believe.

There is a coral reef running the length of the shore which keeps the sharks out (thank goodness) and to which you can walk at low tide if it's full moon. We went with Nevin Kraybills

Mary Harnish and Elizabeth Harnish on vacation at Mombasa with Harnishes, and Nevin Kraybills.

(do you know them?) Probably not. They are a little younger than we are, and I can't get used to the fact that everybody is being so young these days. He is the administrator at Shirati Hospital, and along with Dave's two Aunts, and they insisted on going at full moon and now we know why.

We went surf-boarding—I'm no whiz—and goggling which was fun. We have quite a collection of sea shells now, which we plan to bring home. Maybe we can swap a few with yours from Cape Cod. Mombasa was very **hot** but being at the sea made it bearable. We had to keep all of our fruit locked up because the monkeys came in and ate bananas, oranges, papayas, and any other fruit that was around. They even got into the rice, and spilled my instant coffee jar, which made me very unhappy. It was a thatched roof house and they could get in anywhere. No screens any place, just a wire net type of thing. The night it rained I was glad our beds weren't where the drips were. But the thing that really bothered me was, one day I picked up my tea towel to dry the dishes and I said, "What's this?" It looked like a shrimp all curled up, but here it turned out to be a scorpion! Fortunately I killed it, but I was walking around in the

L to R: Anne Harnish, Elizabeth Harnish, and Rosie Kraybill at Shirati Mennonite missionary station.

night barefoot before that. The others also found one in their refrigerator.

Enough of holidays—I could say yet that we had lobster, which Dave cooked, and also fish which he cleaned and cooked. He did all the suppers which I greatly appreciated. Now we're really packing in earnest. Have about six weeks here yet, and will leave sometime in the middle of May—the exact date is not yet set, but we will leave Nairobi the 25th of May, and arrive in Philly around the first of July. Still wish very much you could take part of this safari with us— it's not too late. It's not too bad traveling with an infant, and we are veterans at it now, at least in East Africa. Come on! I'd like to go to Egypt very much, but don't know if we can dodge all those bullets and bombs, because we also want to go to Israel.

I'm enclosing the driver's license, and would appreciate if you could get it renewed. I have done very little driving here, and I know I'm going to be scared to death in the States. But I don't want to stay at home only! Especially later, when we will probably move out of the city with its easy buses and subways.

Don't have too much else to say. We're fine. Marie said the other day she wishes we could stay for another year. The children are really very good friends with some of the African children now. They are eating the inside of corn stalks (for the sugar content), chew it a while and then spit it out, just like the Africans do. When we ask them if it's clean, they say, "Oh yes, we peel it with our own teeth!" they would much rather squat than sit in a chair, and I don't know what they'll do in school.

I'm trying to wind up my sewing class this week. I feel like I am leaving terribly loose ends. I'm actually just beginning to enjoy the language, and hate to lose that aspect of it.

So much for now. We are eager to see all of you, and especially Beth. Happy birthday, next month, just in case I don't write again. I will bring you a present, but it probably won't arrive for ages and ages since everything will be in the barrels.

Oh yes, the wife of a German missionary who just delivered twins here, asked me if I could ask someone to send her these patterns—Circus Stars to Sew. I said I thought **you** would and she said if you could do that she would appreciate it, and would send you a present of something some time! I had loaned her some of the magazines you had sent me, you see. She has also been reading the La Leche League's Breastfeeding book, and is **very successfully** feeding her twins. She is really different from the other German missionary's wife. Her address is: R-----, Brandt Lutheran Church, Private Bag, P. O. Chimala via Mbeya, Tanzania, East Africa. She knows it will take ages by surface mail.

Love, Flo

P.S. I'm so glad to hear the hemlines are going down! I think.

April 13, 1970

Dear Hiram,

I just want to enclose a small note. We plan to leave here May 15, so don't send anymore official mail here; just keep it in the U.S. until we arrive the end of June.

Could you write me a personal check of $1,800 and send it to me by registered mail? I hope there is enough in the S.&L. for this withdrawal. We need it for the European trip. We are attempting to travel according to Frommer (thanks for the new edition!) on five dollars a day, but with three children it does become a bit expensive. However, we think it will be worth it. When we get our definite schedule, I will send it to you.

I see the debate is still on between recession and inflation. However, it was encouraging to see stocks rise recently.

Do you have a good farm for sale, by chance? We may be interested.

Sincerely, Dave Harnish

VIGNETTES

written 2003-2005

❖ ❖ ❖ ❖ ❖

FIRST ARRIVAL

When we first got to the Ilembula Lutheran Mission station, we were surprised that we wouldn't be living in a mud hut with a grass roof. Actually, before we went to language school in Nairobi, we lived in a house that was the home of a mis- sionary, who was in Sweden with his fam- ily when we arrived. It had several rooms

Anne, Marie, and David playing with a chameleon.

David with chameleon on his head.

added because their family included six children.

The first day we got there, we were so scared. I wanted Dave to help me with the children and unpacking, but he hurried to the hospital—that was his big worry. But later when we had settled in a little bit, we were quite delighted that there were lemon trees growing in the yard. Dave climbed a tree to pick some lemons, and just as he was reaching for one, a snake was on the branch. I guess it wanted lemons too. He got down in a hurry, and got a man from the village to shoot the snake—quite a to-do about it. Also, on the walls, there were big long-legged spiders. I was terrified of them at first, thinking they were probably tarantulas, and would hurt us and the children. Funny about that, though, as time went on, we got so used to those spiders. You just hit the wall a little, and they scurried right up into the attic, where the walls didn't quite meet the ceiling. I remember once writing to my sister, Dora, that the span (legs and all) of one of them was seven inches. I only wrote that for its shock value—we got very used to them. Once there was one behind Dave's wardrobe closet, and I wanted to kill it, but he said it was his pet. That was after we were there a year or so, if I recall.

Another thing we got used to on our walls were the chameleons. In fact, the children played with them. Their camouflage technique was to turn the color of whatever substance they were holding onto. We also found that if their tails were cut off or damaged, they could grow new ones. We didn't have screens on our windows, since we were not in a malarious area. The ants and large cockroaches we never got used to; the millipedes and other bugs were ok if they weren't in the house. Once, one of the Swedish women said she swept a bug off of a porch, and a bit of smoke came out its rear end. "Now I've seen everything," she said.

SINGING CHOIR

Since there didn't seem to be a nursing instructor position open in the hospital school of nursing, I found myself wanting to get to know both the language, so I could talk to people, and to hear the people themselves. I grew weary of people telling me, "The people say this," or "The people think this." I wanted to hear it from "the people" for myself. I diligently studied the language, in Ilembula after our stint in Nairobi at the Language School. I admit to some self pride when I heard from someone (can't remember who) that *Mama Daktari* (Mrs. Doctor) could speak Kiswahili well. I even remember the word: someone asked me when I (a Swedish missionary) would be back from Sweden, and I said (slowly of course) *"Tutamwona atakapofika."* ("We will know when we see her at the time she arrives.") However, I wasn't always so swift in Kiswahili. Once, when we were at our house, I wanted to say, "I will cook potatoes." But instead it came out, "I will cook myself." Bahtletti corrected me, because I had requested it, but she laughed at me a lot too, and we laughed together a lot.

One thing I did do was join (perhaps I was invited, I don't remember) the *wanawake* (women) of the church. I sang in their choir. They had song books only with words in them, no musical notations. One learned the songs from hearing them sung. This choir had about 15 to 20 women in it. As to the songs, I loved them.

I will never forget how dumbfounded and delighted I was to hear *"Gott is Die Liebe"* sung in the Ilembula Lutheran

Tanzanian children on mat.

Church the first time. It was, of course sung in Kiswahili, but there was no mistaking the tune I first learned in German as a small child at Forks Mennonite Church, in Middlebury, Indiana. And, to my amazement, when we returned to the States it had been translated into English in the new Worship Book. Full circle. But when we sing it in our church now, I always sing at least one verse as *"Mungu ni Pendo."* It sounds so much nicer to my ear.

African mothers carry their babies on their backs, even when singing in the choir. I rarely saw a thumb-sucking African baby—if the baby cried, the mother simply swung the child around to the front, and the child sucked on the breast. This was the practice while the mother was singing, too. A breast was for a suckling baby. We have a lot to learn from these women, I decided.

The benches in the large Lutheran Church were made of sun dried mud, and they had no backs. Our children could never sit nicely on the benches as the African children did, to my chagrin. Our children also attended the church's meeting for children, and I learned several of the children's songs from them, which they sang while they were playing. One of them was a "Jesus Loves Me" song, with a totally different type melody: "*Jesu ananipenda*," which I have since taught stateside from time to time. I also learned, from them, not from church, a chant or two. One of them, very catchy, went: "*Maji maji, yakwendapo, maji, maji, yakwendapo*; *Nakwenda polé, polé Nakwende polé, pole.*" (A nonsense phrase that said: "Water, water, where are you going, water water, where are you going; I'm going very slowly, I'm going very slowly.") This was chanted while clapping to the rhythm. Charming.

One time the women were having some kind of religious ceremony. Perhaps it was communion. We sat in a square circle in some kind of little room. There were three things that were very hard for me at that meeting. 1) I was not proficient in the language, especially the religious language, and didn't know what was going on. Also, it might have been in Kibena, the tribal language of the Wabena, among whose tribe we lived; 2) We sat on the ground with our feet straight out in front of us. This was very painful for me to do for any length of time. Even more painful, and perhaps nigh impossible for me, was the squatting position the people took when they sat. I always preferred a chair, and asked for one if there was one available. Sometimes the people just got one for me. They were most gracious and understanding about this. (I think, although who knows what they said when I wasn't there—or was there and couldn't understand.) 3) The third thing that was difficult for me was that we drank some sort of potion. It wasn't *pombe* (the local alcoholic beverage), but perhaps a precursor to it. I will never forget that it was reddish in color, had some kind of grainy stuff in it, AND we drank it from a common cup. It was passed entirely around the group, and when it came to me, it was all I could do to drink it. I knew of the diseases, being a nurse, and the stuff tasted terrible. I can almost feel the nausea now, as I write about it. But I'm glad I drank it; I felt accepted.

FIRE

One evening we discovered that there was a grass fire behind our house. The area between our house and the river was dried grasses, and overgrowth of the *pori* (wild area). Normally, we didn't go through that area much, except taking an occasional walk on a path that went through it. The Tanzanians seemed to go through this area somewhat freely, which was a bit of an amazement to me, since they were mostly barefoot. Occasionally our own children would get into it, then they'd come to me and say, "I was in the tall grass and a snake didn't even bite me!" The Africans usually burnt off the grass before they planted new crops, and this fire got out of hand and came into "our" area. At the time, we thought burning off the grasses was not a good idea, but it does rid the soil of insects, weeds, and other debris not wanted in a cultivated area. I'm not sure if it's a good idea agriculturally or not, but at the time of which I speak, the grasses behind our house were burning, and we had some fear that the fire would reach the house.

So we went out into the "bush" to help put out the flames. Other missionaries and nationals were out there too. As I was beating the fire, I kept thinking, all the snakes and animals are trying to escape the flames too, and here I am, in their path! Strangely, though, after working at extinguishing the flames for a while, these thoughts didn't seem important. Finally the flames were extinguished sufficiently, so that the house was not damaged at all. I can only imagine what would have happened had this type of flame reached a Tanzanian hut with a thatched roof. No more house, at least no more roof.

The concept of "ours" and "yours" was not the same in Ilembula as it had been stateside. I sometimes heard the children playing with other children, and I would hear loud voices, saying, *"Yangu"* (mine), and I thought, children are the same the world over. But the missionaries' ideas differed from that of the nationals. I heard that if an African passed a tree, and there was a mango, or other fruit on it, he would eat some, if he was hungry. But I learned, to my dismay, that not all of the fruit on the mission station was shared in the same way. I had sent my helper, Bahtletti, to pick some oranges from a tree that was near the property of one of the older Swedish missionaries, so I could make some marmalade. I soon heard that I had some nerve to have picked oranges from property that belonged to someone else!

Marie Harnish in guava tree outside our house. I was always uneasy when the children climbed the trees, because we learned snakes could climb trees the first day we arrived at Ilembula.

Regarding trees, especially *maembe* (mango) trees, there would often be small "treelets" growing under the trees. It did take a long time for them to sprout, I think, but there were many. We were not in a lush, lowland, hot growing area—even banana trees did not grow where we lived. A note about that later. We did have *mapera* (guava) trees, and papaya trees, pomegranate trees, and passion fruit, oranges, lemons, and limes. Also possibly many others that I was unable to name. Noteworthy, perhaps, at least to me, was the fact that I didn't know that the fruit that grew on the *mapera* trees were called "guavas" until I returned stateside! Guavas make a beautiful, delicious sauce, much like applesauce, and we ate a lot of it, when guavas were in season. A guava tree grew just outside our house. One always felt like it was applesauce one was going to be eating, but it never tasted quite "right!" One fruit we grew to love were the papayas. With a little orange juice, or lime juice squirted on them, they were delicious! Although, for me, it was an acquired taste, but acquire it I did. One always expected the taste of cantaloupe, but it was not cantaloupe!

Regarding the seedlings that grew under the mango trees, it occurred to me that a grove of these trees could be planted. It was puzzling to me why the Tanzanians didn't plant fruit trees in orchards, such as we did in the U.S. We knew of only one local person that did this, although several of the missionaries had "planted" trees for themselves. So I suggested to the women in my sewing/singing group that they take these little tree seedlings and plant them someplace for themselves. Knowing that water had to be carried from the river for growing things, I suggested that they plant them near the river, or a stream. This action, of planting seedlings, took place shortly before we left. My Kiswahili was pretty good by that time, but many of the women spoke Kibena, not Kiswahili. I have often wondered whether those seedlings grew.

Lake at tea farm. Friends of Ilembula's German missionary.

TEA FARM

One time the German missionary asked us if we would like to accompany her to visit some friends who had a tea farm, some distance away. We responded that we would, and one time we set off on a safari to their place. One thing I remember about that trip, was that it was night, it was several hours away, we were hard pressed to find the place, and the lights in the VW were somehow adjusted so that they shone

On safari, children playing in the lake at tea farm—so rare for them to be able to actually play in water.

up into the trees, rather than on the road, when they were turned on. We did arrive, and there was a lake, the children were allowed to play in it without fear of getting *bilharzia*, and I took the one and only sailboat ride of my life. It was a lovely time. We got very lost on that trip—turned the wrong way most likely, coming home.

VIEW FROM OUR HOUSE

One thing that brought me inspiration and comfort in our home in Ilembula, was the plain that could be seen from our living room window. I purposely arranged the furniture in the room so that one could see out toward the Livingstone Mountains. I have always known that there are two kinds of people—those that like the "coziness" of being surrounded by trees and mountains, and those that need a view of the space(s) surrounding them. For me it is the latter—places where one can see great distances. Perhaps this is a result of growing up in northern Indiana where nothing obscures the landscape in any direction. At least from our window in Ilembula, I liked to sit and look out over the plains. This was a place where one could see the rains coming like sheets, during the rainy season, then hear it thundering on the tin roof. It was a plain that at first glance seemed open and flat, but upon careful perusal, one could see villages, with their thatched roof houses.

SINGING

Sometimes, especially in the evenings, we could hear the nursing students singing. The Tanzanians have an amazing harmony, quite unlike our own. The spaces between the harmony lines were dissimilar to the ones I had grown up with, singing in my home church, Forks Mennonite Church, in Middlebury, Indiana. We grew to love that sound, and the music of Africa always calms me and is beautiful to my ear. I was fascinated by it, and made many recordings of this music. I remember writing to a friend in Philadelphia asking if somehow we could make commercial use of these recordings. One thing about their singing that did amaze us, not the music itself, but the topics they sang about. Coca-cola is everywhere in the world, it seems! Also *Lumumba* (Congo) seemed to be quite a hero in their singing. Also, it seems if the music was indigenous, often one would hear a *kiongozi* (leader) who would line out the song, and the rest would follow. This was especially intriguing to us after the church services. The minister would walk out first, from the front, singing as the *kiongozi,* the congregation would follow him out, and a large circle would be formed with the congregation outside the entrance. The song would end, there would be a prayer, and then the group was dismissed. One song, in particular, which seemed to be indigenous in the Bena area was a song called: *"Nyumbani Ni Yerusalemu"* ("My Home

Nursing students singing in village.

Is in Jerusalem"). It was the first song I learned there, and to this day, I can sing the first verse in Kiswahili, know its meaning, and have translated it into English. When we came home from Tanzania, and lived in the Lancaster area, we were at times asked to give programs for churches. Dave and I, along with our children, would sing this song on our programs, usually after a slide show of various medical ills.

❖ ❖ ❖ ❖ ❖

FLYING DOCTORS

When the flying doctors arrived by plane in Ilembula, it was a momentous thing. For one thing, since Dave was the doctor, we were entitled to feed the visi-

Dave, David, Marie, Florence, and Anne Harnish singing at a presentation following their return to the U.S.

tors. To be able to converse with someone from outside Ilembula was very exciting to me. I remember sitting at our table and talking and talking. One of our children, at first, thought "flying doctors" meant doctors with wings, flying through the air. Of course, they soon became aware that the flying part was in an airplane.

ON THE BUS

Taking a bus trip in Tanzania, was an interesting experience. One takes everything, when one travels by bus. These "everything" objects were loaded onto the top of the bus, and included bicycles, chickens, and luggage, to mention a few things. The buses were piled high, and things were piled on, and tied on. The seats were anything but reclining, and seemed to become harder and harder, especially on one 21-hour trip we took from Dar es Salaam to Nairobi, especially becaue of always needing to hold one child on the lap. If there was a pit stop, it was men on the right, and women on the left. Once a person got on the bus who didn't seem to have the fare necessary, argued with the driver, and the driver deliberately took him past his desired stop so he would have to walk back.

Dave, Anne, and David's twenty-one hour busride from Dar es Salaam to Nairobi in narrow seats.

LOCAL LIFE

It was not at all unusual to see two men walking, holding hands. Never did I see a man and woman walking, holding hands. Perhaps the man wouldn't know which of "his" women to hold hands with? Just about the time we were leaving, there was a movement in the country of "One man, One woman." Don't know what became of this movement, or how successful it was. Certainly the women did the farm work. I have seen entire hillsides that were tilled (hoed) with a *jembe*. I did not see oxen or horses in our part of the country doing the work, only the women. I saw men playing *ubao*, a board game, but I never saw women playing it. The women carried the water from the river on their heads. Near Dodoma, I also saw men carrying water.

I did see women making pots from clay. In fact, I was fascinated by it. There was often a group of them in the area around the church, working, and I often went there to watch them. There was no potter's wheel to be sure, but the pots were as round as could be. They seemed to use shards of pots as their potter's wheel, and their hands were very adept at keeping the pots going round and round as they were forming them. And the pots were beautiful! The decorations were made with a corncob, or an old coin, or whatever could be found at that moment. The pots had rounded bottoms, so they could be set on top of three stones for cooking. I

Women making pottery. Bahtlet, standing, holding Anne Harnish.

know Bahtletti took one of the round "lids" off of our woodburning stove to cook once in a while, and said food tastes so much better if it's cooked in one of the pots. Our children often played that they were making pots. I don't know if they had real clay or mud. The *wanawake* (women) saw how much I enjoyed these pots, and so one time, they came to my yard, and made some pots for ME. Not at my request, but they gave them to me. I treasure those pots, and they are on the mantel in my Ephrata, PA living room. They had put some kind of *dawa* (substance) on them to give them a black border. One is a pitcher, whose handle broke off in shipping it back home, and the other is a "footed" pot. I also have several Tanzanian pots hanging in my home today.

These same pots in my U.S. home which I brought from Africa are mostly hanging from a rope-like arrangement, made for hanging things from trees. In Tanzania, if one puts one's food on the ground, the ants and other *ndudus* (bugs) would soon be in them. I used to think I should do a study on ants, because at different times of the year, different sizes and shapes of ants would come through the house. We had bought a whole stalk of bananas once, and to keep it away from the ants, I thought I would hang the entire stalk from the ceiling in my pantry on a hook that was there. It wasn't long until the ants were crawling down the rope I had hung the stalk on, to get to the bananas!

David, Anne, Marie Harnish. A truck loaded with bananas and pineapples came through Ilembula.

To fire the pots, there was a hole dug in the ground, and they were placed in the hole, upside down. The women gathered dried cow dung, and fired the pots. I know the firing had something to do with the black spots which appeared on the pots. Not the decorative black color, but larger areas. I think the black spots were not fired quite hot enough. Each area, or tribe, had its own particular type or style or decoration on its pots. Beautiful!

This was also true of the baskets. Each tribe had its own style of basket. I have baskets from various tribes—the Wabena, the Wakikuyu, the Wagogo. What beauty the women created, with their hard work. I have a Kikuyu basket that was made by the *aayah* (caretaker) that took care of Anne when we were in language school. I am sure some of the baskets and pots were sold to make money as well.

Speaking of making money, occasionally people would come to our door and try to sell things to us. I wish now I would have been more generous, but at that time we didn't have a lot of money (by U.S. standards), only the MCC living allowance. There would be eggs from a nest found someplace. Once they were tied up in a layette bundle blanket, which had been sent by Mennonites stateside. I also have a little lamp, made from a *copo* (metal can) that may have been obtained from some *wazungus'* trash heap. I can only hope it wasn't from my trash pile. Sometimes they sold fruit, occasionally a truck load of bananas from Mbeya, since we were not a banana-growing area.

In order for the women to earn a little money, I had my sewing class make bead necklaces. They were made of white seeds, about the size of a pea, and small beads that I purchased someplace. For each of these, I would pay them a certain amount of money. They made a lot of them, and I sold them to other missionaries or volunteers. I brought quite a few of these necklaces home, and gave them as gifts to friends and relatives. It was interesting to me to make necklaces from many types of seeds at that time.

Speaking of money, I completely changed my mind on a few things while I was there. Although my Kiswahili didn't allow me to understand all of the religious terms that were used in church there, there was one Sunday when I "got it." The sermon was about Lazarus and the Rich Man. I had always considered myself like Lazarus, not the Rich Man. In that context, in Ilembula, I was suddenly the Rich Man, not Lazarus. This concept has stayed with me. I am very aware, that unless you have seen a true

Lazarus, you do not understand that story. People in the U.S. may think they are poor, but the poorest of the poor have more money than the poorest in some parts of Tanzania.

Another about face I did was regarding black people. Different tribes had different tribal markings on the faces of the women. I heard various stories about how those tribal markings got on the faces of the women, and some were not pleasant stories at all. But we grew to like those tribal markings. They allowed a woman to "belong."

The tribal markings were not what caused the change I made in my own thinking, but rather this: one day I was outside my house and I saw a stranger approach down the dirt road. To myself I thought: "Who is this pasty-faced stranger coming down the path?" *Kumbe*! What did I mean "pasty-faced?" We had been living in a sea of black faces, some of whom were very handsome indeed, both men and women, and I was reacting to a pasty-faced person! It so happens, that it was a new German missionary, a nice enough person, and we were properly introduced. But for myself, I suddenly realized that I no longer had a prejudice against black faces, but an insight into how our faces looked to black people. Thank God. And I do thank God for that insight and growth on my part. For it is true, I was brought up to be prejudiced in my lily-white community in Shipshewana, Indiana.

Along those lines, I had painted a picture of a black woman whom I thought to be particularly beautiful, partly because I wanted to paint, and partly because I did think she was beautiful. I took the painting to Bahtletti, and asked her what she thought of the painting. Bahtletti said (in Kiswahili), "Is she sick?" What a surprise to me. I took the painting and made the person darker! She had appeared pale and sick to Bahtletti.

BUNDLES, JOB'S TEARS, BEAUTIFUL SPOT IN THE WORLD

The differences were striking between the culture we were used to, and what we saw and heard in Tanzanian culture. For one thing, the people for the most part slept on *mkekas* (mats) on the floor. Perhaps that is good for the posture. I don't know. I found these *mkekas* very attractive to the eye. They were hand-woven with various grass-type fibers, no machines. I used a number of them in our house, as floor coverings. Easily picked up, carried, swept under, and kept clean.

Beautiful baskets were everywhere—made with designs and colors which we were told came from roots of plants. Each tribe or location seemed to have hand-woven baskets, with its own unique design. Very, very creative and useful. In the market, though we rarely went to one, there was often a hand-woven bag into which to put one's purchases. I never wanted to destroy these bags—they were so attractive. On one safari , we saw small, plate-sized woven baskets on which to steam fish. Another place we saw a long, large straw with a hand-woven tip with which to drink *pombe* (beer); the tip acting as a sieve. One place where we bought baskets was also one of the most beautiful locations on our earth, in my opinion, at the beginning of the

Rift Valley. It was a very high place where one could look out over the plains for miles and miles. Many of those baskets came home with us, and I gave them to family and friends. I can usually spot a Bena or Kikuyu basket.

Flo Harnish, left, with wanawake (women) from church at Ilembula on Harnish's front verandah. Sewing is done by needle and thread.

Flo Harnish and her sewing group at Ilembula. This was also the beginning of health teaching for the women.

Once, the women were going to have a meeting, close to the river that ran behind our house, and suddenly, they had built a small, card-table size, table for us to use.

The people were obviously poor. When we were in the city, like Dar es Salaam or Nairobi, we would often buy beautiful carvings. At my house in Ilembula, once a woman brought quite a primitive design, a clay "figure" of a woman, but I bought it, and it now sits on my bookshelf and I treasure it.

Once, in a moment I cherish, there were people from a Masai tribe in our village, near the hospital. The Masai are known for their intricate beadings, and were wearing many beautiful necklaces. I could not speak their language at all, but we smiled at each other, and one of the women actually took off her necklace and put it around my neck.

I didn't know whether she was giving it to me, offering it to me to buy, or what. But it was a special moment, and I felt a kinship with her at that moment. Later, I saw one of this Masai group of women and children shaving the eyebrows off of one of her sons—he being about 12 years old or so. There was one thing about the Masai, they are tall, and tend to look straight into your eyes. The Bantu people, among whom we mostly lived, were shorter, and tended to look down, not directly into your eyes.

Mother with sick child in shared bed at Ilembula Lutheran Hospital.

A difference I particularly noted, since I am a registered nurse, was that when a child was ill, and a patient in the hospital, the mother would sleep in the same bed with the child. What a lot we have to learn from the Bantu. When I was a student, many years ago, we were "taught" to ask the parents to leave the room when a particular procedure was to be done to the child, and particularly at night—no parents were allowed to stay. We did not comprehend that the child was too afraid to act out if the parents weren't around. Now that perception in nursing has changed, I realize. Also, patients' families cooked their meals for them—thus ensuring the patients received the foods they liked.

One day, it was decided that some of the things from the storeroom sent by MCC (and other donors)

Cooking area of the hospital. Relatives are cooking food for the patients they have brought.

People waiting and looking in window at the storeroom during the handing out of bundles and other items from the United States.

would be given out to the people. For one thing, a few of the things were getting moldy. There had also been a number of break-ins to the storeroom and the concept of giving the items as inducements to come to the hospital didn't totally work. At least that was my understanding of it. So the word went out that some things were to be given freely to people. What a day! Hunger, or greed, or a gimme mentality was rampant. One item at a time was given—I know some mothers sent their children through the line as often as they could, just to get an item—a belt, perhaps, a small layette blanket, perhaps, or just about anything. I was shocked to see all of this. I am no longer sure what my own role was in that proceeding, but it was not a blessed scene.

SEMOLINA

For breakfast, we often ate a cream-of-wheat-like cereal, made from Semolina (Cassava). This Semolina often had bugs in it. By way of confession, I usually took out the bugs, knowing they would not hurt my family, but it was usually too much for me, myself, to eat that cereal!

TOYS

The Tanzanian children, and possibly adults, were very clever in toys that they made. They had cornstalks, so they would make very elaborate trucks with the pulp of the cornstalk, and hold it together with the long, sharp thorns from the thorn trees. Tin from any source was used, and these toys were quite impressive. The thorns were like nails, to be sure. We wore flip-flops much of the time, and these thorns pierced the flip-flops completely. Sometimes we saw more sturdy flip-flops made of old tires. These could not be pierced by thorns. Most people, however, went barefoot. I am sure it was this type of cruel thorn that made the crown Jesus wore on the cross.

UNICEF SEWING MACHINE

The sewing machine I used in Tanzania was a UNICEF sewing machine. Why it was there, in my house, I don't know. I have always done a lot of sewing for myself and the children, so it was put to good use. At first, I didn't know how I would ever operate a machine that used one hand just to turn the wheel. But it was amazing—it didn't seem too difficult after a while, and I did a lot of sewing on it. Not like the old treadle machine my mother used when I was young, but it certainly did the trick of sewing. Of note, in some areas, the clothes of the children of the country were the same color as that of the earth, probably because it was the only set of clothing the child had.

❖ ❖ ❖ ❖ ❖

VISIT TO SHIRATI

One time mid term we thought we would take a little visit to Shirati in northern Tanzania. It looked like it was about a day's drive on the Shell map Aunt Mary had sent us even before we went to Tanzania. We had our VW Bug that we had purchased in Nairobi, and we all fitted into it nicely. I think we were on our way to a TAP Retreat at Limuru, which was in Kenya, and still in East Africa, so this would be a good time to visit relatives.

We started out, happily. I remember as we followed the map we came to the *pori* (open area or wild area) and just followed the tracks. No paved roads there, of course, just two tracks, but definitely a road or trail. I particularly remember we were singing with the children, and one of the songs we were singing was "Bobby Shafto's gone to sea, he'll come back and marry me, silver buckles on his knee, pretty Bobby Shafto." Why I remember that piece of trivia I'm not sure, but whenever I hear it, I think of that particular safari. There are other trivial things I remember, and other important things I don't remember, but I remember singing that song over and over. I also remember one of the children requesting "He Leadeth Me" from Dave and it was indeed an appropriate song to sing on that particular safari. Another thing I remember from the early part of that trip is that we saw an ostrich

On safari, VW Bug going to Shirati.

with a dozen babies. We counted them. We were delighted to see such a sight and drove off into the grassy *pori* to follow them a bit. It was a bit of a lark, quite unlike what came later.

With VW Bug on Safari: L to R: Anne, Marie, David, Flo, helping David with shirt.

After a while, the two ruts that were the road, occasionally were muddy, and occasionally there were even big puddles, and as we went along BIGGER puddles. Then, all we could see was water, everywhere, hardly any tracks at all. Early in the *pori* we met a LandRover, with one person in it. I thought at the time we passed each other that he had looked at us kind of "funny." But lots of things in Tanzania were kind of funny. I do remember as we got through some of the larger puddles, I grew very tense at times, being afraid we'd get stuck in the mud yet once again! After a while it became only water, and Dave decided we'd better investigate ahead. We had also passed one native hut and *rondovel*, but hadn't seen any more for a long time. According to the map, it really wasn't that much farther at all.

I think Dave was extremely brave at that time. He got out of the VW, took a sturdy stick, took off his shoes, rolled up his pant legs, and walked out in that water to see how deep it was, testing with the stick. I know I wouldn't have had the courage to do that! Snakes, *bilharzia*, and who knows what else could be in that water! He disappeared from sight for a while, and when he came back, he said, "There's a big river up ahead!"

What to do. Going back seemed impossible through all of that mud we had barely slid through, and we were just about out of petrol. We decided to go back a little way to the hut and, what must have been a park ranger, and ask him what to do. We got to the hut, and the ranger said sometime tomorrow (*kesho*) a plane would come and bring us petrol. So we went into the little hut, which had one single bed, with a very torn mosquito net, as well as holes in the sides of the hut. I had, by that time, learned to take needle and thread with me, as well as water and a little food. But we had very little water, and very little food, because we thought we would soon be there. It was nighttime, so I mended the mosquito net, I remember it got very small when I had mended all the holes. I can't remember who slept in the bed, but probably all of us. The children were still very young at that time. I stuffed shirts and under-pants in the holes in the wall.

I remember the man, maybe a woman too, and def-initely a child, brought us some hot British-style tea the next morning, and it tasted wonderful. We had our camera along, and he asked us if we would take a picture of his son. Of course we agreed to that, so he said to wait, and he would put the best clothes on the son. When the child returned he had on a shirt and shoes—nothing else. We took the pic-ture, got his address, and later sent it to the family.

We began to realize that *kesho* could mean tomorrow, or next week, or possibly next month. Dave and I conferred, to decide what to do. No one knew where we were. That was really dumb of us not to let someone from Ilembula know where we were. Aunts Mary and Elizabeth Harnish were expecting us the next day, although they knew delays could happen in that coun-try. We decided we had to make it back—that is, Dave decided. I depended on him for decisions like that at that time.

So we started back, and although I dreaded going through those pools of water where we almost got stuck, we did it, and we made it. Someplace we must have gotten petrol, and went the long way around. It was not so easy that way either. We were traveling in the rainy season, and anybody that had been in that country for a while, knew that you shouldn't try to do what we had tried. Some of the road that we took was paved, but again nightfall came before we arrived at our destination. When it's night in Africa, it's dark! So we drove until we saw lights again, and that was a Catholic Hospital. That night we slept in the delivery rooms of the hospital. It was a better night than the night before. Something to laugh about.

As we safaried on, we came to a deep washout. There was no way we could get across the ravine below. So we did what one has to do, and "hired" some local persons to push us through on a round-a-bout (of our own making). I remember it was deep, and that it was raining. The local people had gathered, and were using giant banana leaves as umbrellas.

It was always a bit hairy while traveling, to stop and take a mandatory pit stop. It would seem to us that there were no houses or people around, but in a few minutes they would gather. If you needed to empty your bladder, etc., it was necessary to do it very quickly indeed. As for the nationals, they were not quite as bent on privacy as we were, and we often saw men voiding along the road, watching us, and we watching them. Once I saw a woman with a huge load of wood on her head, who simply urinated as she was stopped and did not unload. I also learned it was better to go in the bush than in the Asian-style *choos* (toilets), especially with children, because some people's aim was not good.

Speaking of travelling with children, we usually had to stop at borders of countries—Kenya and Uganda—and have our luggage checked. I learned from a friend to put a dirty diaper on top. No disposables in those days. It speeded up the process.

We did finally arrive at Shirati, three days after we had intended to. Only greenhorns would have taken the road we took during the rainy season. Live and learn.

MEETING NYERRE

I don't know if the time we had the car trouble is the time we were returning from Dar es Salaam or perhaps from Dodoma. I can't remember if we stayed at Schillers, the Lutheran Guest House, or The Salvation Army Guest House. If we stayed at the

Salvation Army Guest House, what I primarily remember about that place was that it was HOT! It was a series of thatched roof round houses, with no fans. And of course the mosquito nets to sleep under. But we were used to mosquito nets, and welcomed them. Dar, of course, was malaria country, being at sea level. If there were nets, I am sure I mended them. I mended a lot of mosquito nets in my stay in Tanzania.

If we stayed at the Lutheran Guest House, it was pure luxury to us! I know we always wanted ice cream when we went to Dar, because we never had any at Ilembula, although I think I did try to make some once in our kerosene refrigerator's ice tray, with Aunt Mary's recipe. As I recall, that ice cream turned out more like an "ice" than ice cream. Also, in Dar, it would have been lovely to go swimming, and we did walk on the beach some. But the beach, and the water, and most everything else was covered with thick grease. When we would return from the beach, our feet were loaded with grease. We never went in the water there. We did see large ocean-going ships there, which was fascinating.

If we stayed with Schillers, and we probably did on the occasion I want to write about, it was lovely, and they were most hospitable. Dar es Salaam being at sea level and Ilembula being in the southern Highlands at an elevation of about 4,400 ft. above sea level, there was also quite a contrast to what we were used to, weather-wise. But Schillers had large fans above the beds, and it made sleeping and being there quite tolerable, although not as comfortable as we were used to at Ilembula.

The reason I think we were at Schillers was because we went to a Christian Medical Society meeting while we were in Dar. Maybe that's why we went, I can't remember. But we went to a party or meeting

View of plains from southern highlands in Tanzania. Beginning of the Rift Valley.

of the CMS, and I know our children were not at the meeting. We must have left them with our gracious host and hostess, the Schillers.

We were at the meeting and the main speaker was Nyerre, the president of Tanzania. We were quite impressed with him and his concepts for the country of Tanzania. We shook his hand, joined a group in conversation that was always around him, and all in all felt very good about this encounter. Someone said, I can't remember who, that Nyerre would stand on any street corner like a schoolboy and expound and argue about his ideas. It was during this time that he espoused the concept of "UJAMAA." Something to the effect that each village should live and work together, have a house for guests, and it would mean great progress for the country. In the countryside, we heard a lot of complaints about this system, although I think for the most part, the problem was, as everywhere, people did not want sweeping changes. We were not directly involved in this process, but thought it a good idea.

At any rate, after this most interesting of CMS meetings, as we left we were on something of a high. However, I felt that I suffered great indignity personally, when I had to push our VW Bug to get it started! That seemed to be standard procedure for the Bug, at that time. At least I remember going out and pushing it, and Dave sitting in the car starting it. Maybe he pushed a bit, then jumped in—let's hope so. We probably had our children, those that were old enough, also help to push it at other times to get it started. But I have frequently complained and told the story about shaking the hand of the president of the country, and then suffering the indignity of having to push my car to get it started! Actually, in that country, we were lucky to even have a car!

A TENSE TIME

One of the most tense moments I spent while in Tanzania was after our car, the VW Bug, developed motor failure. We depended on that car, spent several nights sleeping in it, and though it gave us problems, we also came to know its capabilities and incapabilities. We did know it "floated" across water-filled roadways rather easily, with a little help from those pushing it, that it was very uncomfortable to spend nights in, but it was a constant companion. We always traveled with water, food, and mosquito nets for opening the windows, after the first unhappy fateful night we spent in the car.

On our way home from a safari to Dar es Salaam, the car began to make a terrible noise, and we thought it would stop on us any minute. There was something horrendously wrong with it, but we managed to slowly limp some miles into Iringa with it. We left the car there to be fixed, and took the bus from Iringa to Ilembula. The problem for me, though, was when we were let off at the stop to Ilembula, there was no one to get us, and, of course there was no way to notify anybody that we were even arriving. This was at night, and the nights in Africa are dark, indeed. There are no lights. "Dark night" has a different meaning in an area with no lights, than it does in the U.S.

The place where the bus stopped for Ilembula was about two miles from our home there. The Tanzanians do walk around at night, at times, but we didn't. Occasionally, Dave would need to go to the hospital at night, and use our large, trusty flashlight to light the path. We never went anyplace on safari or any travels without this large squarish flashlight, and I do remember it with fondness. It was even waterproof, and one of our prize possessions. This night, in my memory, was cloudless, and starless. How were we, with three small children, at that time, ages 6, 4, and 1, going to get to our house in that pitch dark night?

Getting to the station and to our house involved crossing a deep gorge, with a wooden bridge made of a series of boards or planks, with no sides on it, which allowed vehicles and pedestrians to cross. The gorge was about 25 feet in depth over the river in the dry season. When it was the rainy season, of course, the river rose quickly and became a raging torrent. This was in the dry season.

After getting off the bus, with our children and luggage, we found a half-demolished, mud dried-brick house. There was no roof on it, but there was a corner left. Sun-dried mud brick was the standard material of houses in that area, although our house and some of the other missionaries' houses were made of kiln-dried brick. If left to themselves, and not kept up, the mud houses disintegrated in time. Such was the one we found. It was pitch dark in it. We cleared a corner, or sat in a corner that was more clear. The children and I were huddled as close together as we could get, while Dave needed to walk to the village, get the Landrover and come back and get us. Dave showed great courage that night. I really don't think I personally could have done it. He walked through the *pori*, across the bridge (no railing on the bridge of course), and into the village to get the Landrover.

While we waited, which seemed interminable, I was about as tense as you can get. There I was, with my three young children, in the dark, in poisonous snake country. In order to save the battery, I would turn on the flashlight to see if any snakes were there only every so often. I tried to reassure the children that we were safe, and that Daddy would soon be back. I tried to remember that snakes don't attack you unless they are attacked. To no avail. I don't think I have ever had greater tension than in those few hours as I sat in the corner of that broken down hut with my children, waiting for their father to come. And never have I been happier to see someone, than when he came with the LandRover. Dave, himself, recalls that there was some moon that evening, as he crossed the railless bridge.

Minister, as kion-gozi, *leading congregation out after church service. While they all are singing, the congregation forms a large circle outside and are then dismissed following prayer.*

KANISA HUKO ILEMBULA
(The church in Ilembula)

At the mission station where we were, there was of course, a Lutheran Church. And we did travel some in Lutheran circles. But I missed the Mennonite circles so much. The church building was a big (to me) Lutheran structure. The benches were made of sun-dried mud, without backs. Birds flew in and out of the windows. We were always a little embarrassed because our children didn't sit still, like it seemed the Tanzanian children did. Perhaps all parents, everywhere, have these thoughts. But we attended every Sunday, walking up a little hill. The sermons were a little hard to grasp with our relatively limited religious Kiswahili, although that improved as time went on. We thought the church rather large in an area where there were only huts with grass roofs. We ourselves had a *mabati* (tin) roof.

Above: Inside the Lutheran Church at Ilembula—birds frequently flew through the church. Left: Lutheran Church fifty miles from Ilembula.

In our house, in Ilembula, Bahtletti did the laundry on a wash board. There was no washing machine there. The village women did their laundry on a stone at the river. I know I never wanted Bahtletti to put our laundry away after it was washed, ironed, and folded. I didn't want her to see all of the clothes we had! Once, at one of our TAP Retreats, I asked about this, because it was bothering me about all of the toys and things our children had. The response from one of our leaders was that that was a cultural necessity for our children to have those things. Perhaps. I don't know. To this day, when I have such a beautiful home, the water gushes out of the tap, I wash my hands before touching food—I think about those strong women who carry water in big 5-

or 10-gallon debbies on their heads, having obtained the water from the river and walking miles to their homes, as well as big loads of wood on their heads besides the baby on the back, and perhaps one in the womb. And I wonder how one can teach them sanitation in terms of washing their hands, even. The children there died in a high (I've forgotten their exact mortality number) rate from the diarrheas and other preventable diseases.

In the church, when the offering was taken, I think about once a year or so, there would be big baskets of corn carried up to the front of the church, or perhaps beans, or some other commodity grown locally. Women were usually making pottery outside the church during the week to sell for the church. I heard it said, since polygamy was practiced there, women were allowed to join the church, but not polygamous men. True? I'm not sure.

BAHTLETTI'S
LEAVING

I had always heard that the Africans don't tell you directly what's on their minds about what they were going to do. As usual, I was skeptical of what other people said that Africans do. However, once (at least) it did happen to me. One day Bahtletti, after having worked for us so capably for a couple of years, asked me what I would think about a certain matter. She said, "What if Hilkka's house girl would be leaving, but Hilkka wouldn't know about it?" I really thought it a strange question, and I can't remember what I responded—probably that the house girl should tell Hilkka. I'm not sure why I remember this conversation, but it did seem significant at the time. But, sure enough, Bahtletti herself told me sometime later that she, herself, was leaving to get married. I was sad, and angry, that she could "abandon" us like that. I depended on her for so many things. For the laundry, fires, conversation, occasionally cooking, and in general being a lifeline to my stay in Ilembula. I had grown very dependent on her. I did manage to get another house girl, but it was not easy.

Picture of Bahtlet, getting married. Picture was sent to us.

SAFARIS

Another safari we took, I don't remember where we were going, maybe just to take a trip, but we had a very bad mishap in that it rained and we couldn't go ahead because of the road and we couldn't go back because of the road. So that meant a night in the VW. What a terrible night! Five people in a VW Bug! Dave would put our suitcases on top of the car, to make as much room for us as possible inside the car. We usually put the mosquito netting in the open window, then slammed the door shut so we could get some air, but not be all bitten up by mosquitoes. We had begun to carry food and water with us wherever we went (learned that the hard way), and would try to situate ourselves and get some sleep. Anne usually fared the best, because she could be placed way in the back behind the back seat, and stretch out. Dave and I made out the best we could in the front seats, and Marie and David the same in the back. The children didn't mind it as much as Dave and I did, especially me.

On this particular safari, during the night, because I couldn't sleep, I saw small lights that darted here and there, all around the car. I thought it was like a cat's eyes, when you see their eyes at night, they sometimes gleam, if the lights of the car hit them just right. But, I thought these were lions' eyes! I thought there were lions all around our car, just waiting to devour us, if we dared step outside. I remember waking Dave and telling him about the lions' eyes. He apparently slept better than I did. We also heard snorting and other kinds of noises, which I am at a loss to explain. We had parked the car in the only remaining spot, beside a river, and thought that the rain and mud might make us slide right into the river. What a terrible night!

In the morning, we could see no lions. All we could see was mud, mud, mud. Ahead of us, although we were returning, was a big sea of mud where the road usually ran. All around us we could see hippo tracks, although there were no hippos evident in the daylight. To be sure, they probably were there, as well as in the river. I remember on that

Anne and Flo on safari.

trip, Dave's bravery and ingenuity were apparent. We had to get out of there, but how? The road ahead was totally mud, the road behind us was washed out. So Dave, again, took off his shoes and socks, and in order to make the car as light as possible, carried the suitcases one by one by hand through the mud, then carried the children through the mud, then came back, took my

Top: Left to Right: David Harnish, Felicia Fabricius, Flo and Anne Harnish, Mrs. and Mr. Fabricius. The Fabricius' were the nearest Americans, 60 miles away. Bottom Left: Rice paddies sponsored by U.S., and managed by an American couple, 60 miles from Ilembula in Ruaha. Bottom Right: Harnish children at Ruaha River on vacation.

hand, and led me through the mud. I had to be barefoot, also, that time. Then he went back and brought the car through the mud. I remember holding my breath as he slithered and slid through that mud.

After that night in the car, and through the mud, we came, after a little while, to a tourist place, and went in and got something to eat. I remember the terrible, troubled, dirty feeling we had, and then we got into this wonderful place where there was food, and the incomprehension they had of how we had spent the previous night. Later, we also learned that what I thought were lion's eyes, were actually some kind of butterfly or bird that flies in the night, much like our fireflies in the states.

Another safari we took was to the Ruaha, which was just being developed as a game park. We went with an American couple, who lived about sixty miles from Ilembula. They had a child, approximately the age of Marie. We needed to cross the Ruaha River on a ferry, so we drove our car right onto the ferry, and went over with it. I knew there were crocodiles in the river, and I kept the children as close to myself and the car as I could. That ferry was more like a raft, with no sides.

When we got to the game park, there were some buildings, but we cooked outside. I remember being at the cooking place, can't remember what I was making for dinner, when I saw elephants running. When you see a herd of elephants running, they don't seem to be going very fast, but they are. We had seen several herds of elephants walking by the buildings, and usually we just moved into a building, or car, or someplace to get out of the way until they passed through. But I later was told, by Dave, that he and our friend had wanted to see how close they could get to the elephants to take pictures, but the elephants began to chase them. Dave said he was scared, and ran into the building to get away from the elephants.

We took several safaris to game parks to see animals. It is a little like bird-watching. When a leopard, lion, hyena, gazelle, wildebeest, giraffe, or other animal is spotted, everyone gets very excited, gets out their camera, and brags about their find. The trips to the game parks were often dusty, long, and tedious—but very rewarding.

Once, I decided I would stay in the *rondovel*, rather than go into the LandRover to hunt (with cameras) the animals. That was a very lovely decision. While I was in the *rondovel*, I saw elephants playing on the banks of a river in the sand. They wanted acacia buds to eat, so they would go up to a huge tree, push it to make it shake, and the acacia buds would fall down, and they could eat them. It was a wonderful sight. I also saw a large herd of wild buffaloes come to the water to drink. Usually, when we saw buffaloes, we were very careful, because they could charge, and be dangerous. But this was the most serene scene one could want. They all put their heads down, and drank from the river. On this trip, I felt I had been

On safari in Serengeti—a leopard in the tree.
A sight to get excited about in the LandRover.

rewarded by staying in the *rondovel*, while everyone else was in a hot, dusty LandRover, trying to find animals.

On another trip, during the dry seasons, Dave wanted to shave in the morning. We were aware that if elephants need water in the dry season, they dig a hole in a river bed, and get water that way. Well, that's what Dave did. He dug a hole in the bottom of a dry river bed, got some very muddy water to shave with, and shaved. He was proud of himself, although I thought it rather ridiculous.

A STRESSFUL TIME

One Sunday afternoon we were taking a walk on a path toward the river behind our house in Ilembula. Most other days of the week, Dave was busy in the hospital with patients, teaching, and other activities he did there. Our son, David, stumbled, and when he got up he began to cry loudly. That didn't seem so unusual for a child, but the crying didn't stop as usual, and he cried and cried. David, being about four years old, began annoying us with the continuousness of the complaints. However, after some time of this, Dave took a close look at his eye, and found that one of the needle-like projections from the tip of the three foot (or so) grasses had pierced the cornea of his eye, and was still lodged there.

This was alarming, and we took him up the hill to the hospital. Dave had determined that the projection needed to be removed, both because it was giving our son continuous pain, and because fluid from the vitreous or aqueous humor of the eye might leak out, and cause trauma to his eye.

Dave called the Swedish nurse to come and give the anesthesia. By this time, I was becoming quite anxious about our son. The projection was safely removed, and David wore a big bandage on his head to provide pressure to prevent leakage of the fluid(s) for a period of a week or so. Fortunately, no permanent damage to our son's eye was done.

TANZANIAN CUSTOMS & RETURNING HOME

To be called *Mzee* (old man) was a title of great respect. Even a young person who deserved to be honored, could be called *Mzee*. Another custom in our area of Tanzania was to call a woman by the name of her first child. For example, one woman was called "Mama Fexus," because that was the name of her oldest child. I could have been called "Mama Marie," since that was the name of my oldest child. However, I remember mostly being called "*Mama Daktari*" (Mrs. Doctor). Stateside, I have also been called "Mrs. Dr. Harnish." (The wife of a title!)

One thing that happened among other things, is that I asked Bahtletti what she wanted when I went away—*i.e.*, came back to the U.S. Or maybe it was at the time that she left and got married. She said she would like my *sufarini*. I thought that meant the very thin kettles I bought in Tanzania, but I now think she meant my heavier cooking pots. This is where my Kiswahili failed me. I was not able to comprehend what it was that she wanted, although we discussed it several times. I have brought home several of the small cooking pots I bought and used there, and I use them here. But I always feel some guilt at not having understood Bahtletti about the cooking pots. We Americans have so many things, and that might have made life a little easier for her, although I don't think she was one of the poorest of the poor.

As Dave and I were thinking about going home, since our three years' time was about up, I had mixed emotions. For one thing, as we were heading to Tanzania from Philadelphia, I wondered what effect it would have on our children to live in a foreign land. At no time did I think we would be inadequate to care for them (perhaps I should have), but what effect would the country have on them. After all, we were United States citizens, we had had friends in Philadelphia, next door neighbors who had adored them as much as though they were their own grandchildren, and family— although family was at some distance, on both Dave's side and my side. Now, in leaving Ilembula, I was surprised to feel that I was wondering what effect it would have on our children to uproot them from where they had lived, apparently very happily, for three years, and go back to the U.S. where everything would be so different. I don't think I really considered what effect it might have on me or Dave—rather short-sighted to be sure.

One day there was some kind of ceremony at the hospital because of Dave's leaving. I was there too, but didn't think it had much to do with me. I remember being bored, and not knowing what was going on, and probably resenting that I had not been part of the hospital work.

I had gained 50 lbs., and was not at all happy about it. I didn't realize then, that I would continue this weight gain, and have deeper depression when we came back. This is indeed what did happen to me, but at the time of leaving Tanzania, I was thinking mostly of the children.

A few weeks before we left Ilembula, something significant did happen to me. Some customs I was not used to. It was considered very bad "manners" (in some way—maybe like picking your nose in public stateside) to hand someone something with your left hand. Certainly it was not bad manners to pick your nose there—it was done openly and constantly, and there were many runny noses. It was also the custom of women in that country to curtsy (a legacy of the British rule?) when they encountered a man, or someone of importance. And if that was a person of great importance, the women would actually kneel. The curtsying, actually seemed rather attractive, but the kneeling always left me feeling angry that one person would kneel to another. But near our house, on the way going up the hill towards the hospital, a woman kneeled to ME! She was saying something, but I couldn't understand it. Probably it was in Kibena. I didn't know what to do with that kneeling. Finally, I got down on my knees, and kneeled, also. This may have been an "incorrect" thing to do, but it was what I did. As I have considered this through the years, I believe that she was thanking me for something. I don't know what it was for, but I have cherished the memory. Perhaps my being in Africa did mean something to some one person after all. That is the way I shall remember it, and give myself comfort, even though I did not do the nursing work I would have liked to do. I felt greatly honored and respected by this kneeling. This incident is fixed in my memory, and I pray that that woman remembers me with love, as I remember her with love.

However, to be honest, there were times when I would gladly have given up the opportunity to be in Ilembela. We were placed in a situation in which there was no one to go to for personal help or confidences. If our marriage had problems, they were accentuated. Many were the times when I, we, could have used help. I was so lonely, and Dave was so busy, and perhaps frustrated along with it. We had plenty of arguments and disagreements, to be sure. I feel that few marriages could have withstood the tensions we were dealing with at that time and I praise God that since that time we have been able to negotiate our needs and differences, and we truly, deeply care for each other. I do think our situation could have been ameliorated by more careful planning by the sending agencies, as well as by us. We did not have a supporting church at the time, and were sent to another denomination as well, putting us quite in limbo. Would we have related better in a Mennonite setting, or perhaps with more Americans nearby, or perhaps with an assignment for me? Only God knows.

ARRIVING HOME

When we got home to Philadelphia, we returned to our house at 111 Elfreth's Alley. Dave did not know where he would go to set up a medical practice. He explored many local places, and some at a distance, traveling, and occasionally staying overnight to take calls, or because the distance was so great.

Finally, he settled on a practice with a good opening requiring a surgeon, in the Akron-Ephrata area in Pennsylvania. It was propitious. I already had family from Indiana in the area, two brothers; Rollin and his wife Betty Stutzman Rheinheimer with their family, and Howard and his wife Miriam Miller Rheinheimer with their family. We house hunted, and found a house that both of us liked. Our friends and realtors, Hiram and Mary Jane Lederach Hershey, helped us with the purchase. It was located in Akron, PA, and was near Mennonite churches. We visited around to find a church home that would fit us. I remember visiting one Mennonite church of the area, and when it came to Sunday School, they asked me how old I was, so I could be placed in the correct women's class! I never went back there. What does age have to do with church?

The Mennonite church in Akron seemed very suitable to me. My brother, Rollin, and his family were already attending there, and it seemed a lot like the churches in Indiana that I had grown up in, like at Forks (at Middlebury) or Goshen College. Dave and I were not in total agreement at first as to which church to attend. He had been a member of a Lancaster Conference Church, so there was quite a bit of difference in worship style, dress, and other matters—some of which seemed stifling to me. But the Akron church! Oh, how wonderful I thought it was. I had been so lonely in Tanzania for friends, and in this church it seemed you could have all the friends you wanted! Think me crazy, perhaps, to me there seemed to be a virtual physical glow/halo over the church. We started attending, and eventually asked for membership, as did our three children, as they grew older.

Once, however, I remember in a Sunday School class, in some discussion, persons were giving their experiences regarding some issue. Mercifully, I have forgotten who said it, but when I said, "The Africans do it this way . . ." Someone responded with, "I don't want to know what the Africans do. I want to know what they do here." That did shut me up, and contributed to the depression and reentry problems I was facing. I know I have also said things in like manner, unwittingly, and hurt someone's feelings. But my experience had indeed just been in Africa, and I felt, and still feel that we have a lot to learn from our African sisters and brothers.

Return from Africa. Picture taken at Dave's parents' home in Lancaster, PA, 1970. Left: Laura Reinhardt Rheinhemer and Ed Rheinheimer, Flo's parents; Right, Esther Miller Harnish and Clarence H. Harnish; Center: David M. Harnish and Florence Rheinheimer Harnish, with children David, Anne, and Marie Harnish. Note Tanzanian clothes made by Flo and worn by Flo, David and Anne.

I have been changed in my entire world view by this wonderful/terrible experience—I am truly grateful that God loves the imperfect people on this earth, like me.

PHOTOS

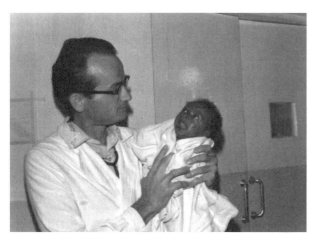

A baby delivered by Dr. David Harnish, named: "Harnish".

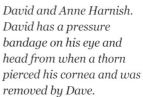

Bahtlet carrying her baggage on her head.

David and Anne Harnish. David has a pressure bandage on his eye and head from when a thorn pierced his cornea and was removed by Dave.

Hospital UNICEF Landrover and Tanzanian children.

Dave and Anne Harnish examening donated spectacles.

Ilembula Lutheran Hospital

Ilembula Lutheran Hospital

Medical clinic close to hospital at Ilembula.

People waiting for medical services at Ilembula Lutheran Hospital.

Mother and child waiting at Ilembula Lutheran Hospital.

Dave, Landrover, and navigation problems.

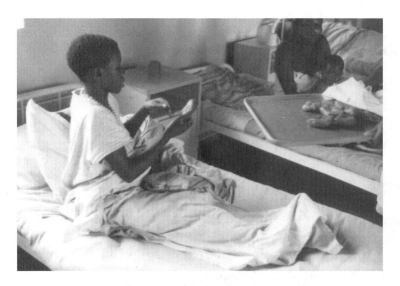

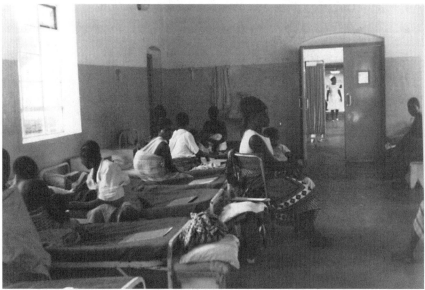

Patients inside Ilembula Lutheran Hospital (top and middle).

Partially collapsed roof on house after heavy rains. Dave Herr, M.D., (visiting from U.S.) standing to right.

Dr. and Mrs. David Herr, with Harnish and Herr children.

David Herr on safari, standing in a cave, behind the waterfall and looking out at the waterfall. This was near a leprosarium which we visited.

Typical house near Ilembula.

A house made of bamboo in a banana growing area of Tanzania.

Man in front of house, made of bamboo, mud, grasses.

House near Wagogo area, Tanzania.

Graveyard at Ilembula.

Dave and Flo Harnish, Marie, Anne and David.

Tanzanian boys with fish.

A hive for bees. Wild bees could be a serious problem if they attacked eople or animals.

Tanzanian watoto (children) playing.

Tanzanian children.

*Anne and David Harnish amongst
fowl raised by Dave in Ilembula.*

Tanzanian mother and child.

Marie Harnish learning to make a basket by unidentified woman.

Anne Harnish sleeping with dolls. Note homemade crib.

Anne Harnish, 3rd birthday— pillow in background made in Shirati.

Youth near Ilembula.

Bahtlet hanging out laundry.

Dave cutting David's hair.

*Charles (left), "Shamba boy", with Anne Harnish.
Charles is working in garden.*

David, Dave, Marie holding Anne Harnish. In front of thatched roof house close to our house in Ilembula. This house was later torn down.

Harnish House peddlers. Eggs tied up in layette blanket.

Swedish missionary Ingegard Troedson, with David, Anne, and Marie Harnish in Ilembula.

Harnish miniature collie in Ilembula.

Right: Anne, Marie, and David Harnish in Ilembula

Left: Dave, Anne, David and Marie Harnish playing at Ilembula.

Marie Harnish with friend in 1970.

Anne, David, Marie Harnish on front porch, Ilembula. Swedish missionary child at left.

A homemade seesaw in Ilembula—David and Marie Harnish enjoying it.

Anne Harnish on swing while visiting Flo's brother in Kenya. Dave was climbing Mt. Kilimanjaro. Bonnet made by Dave's mother, Esther Harnish.

L to R: Bahtlet, David and Anne Harnish, Charles washing Max, the dog, to rid him of ticks. Marie Harnish, middle right, and Swedish missionary children.

David and Anne Harnish, held by Ralph Rheinheimer; Randy and Lisa Rheinheimer to right. In Kenya at Rheinheimer home.

On safari in Serengeti, herd of water buffalo.

At right, typical way of carrying a child. Unidentified, near Ilembula.

Flo Harnish with children Anne, David and Marie at Lutheran Guest House in Dar es Salaam, Tanzania.

Clearing field for flying doctors.